CONTENTS

INTRODUCTION

From rockets that can fly at more than **20,000 miles an hour** to a motorbike with only one wheel, machines can be brilliant or bonkers – and sometimes even both.

The longest ship ever built, the heaviest digger and the largest aeroplane, the world's first working motor car, and its most expensive one. What machines like these have in common is that they all say a lot about the inventiveness and imagination of the people who conceived and created them.

Designed to drive faster, fly higher, carry more cargo or – in the case of space rockets – travel hundreds of thousands of miles to places no one has ever been before, not every idea has worked but the best have been inspired and inspirational, and in a few cases they have gone on to change the world.

When Karl Benz built the world's first automobile more than **130** years ago he couldn't possibly have known that one day there would be more than a billion motor vehicles running on roads that stretch for literally millions of miles.

Similarly, America's decision to send a handful of astronauts to the Moon eventually needed the talent and expertise of an incredible **400,000** men and women to make it happen. Just imagine: **400,000** scientists, engineers and mathematicians who together spent more than ten years designing, building and flying the mighty Saturn V rocket.

With more than three million parts, their creation was easily the most expensive, most complicated machine ever made. But many other machines are still remarkable despite being small and relatively simple.

The world's tiniest jet, for example, does more than **300 miles an hour** yet can be towed behind a car and parked in the garage. Another modern flying machine, the Albatross, was constructed using plastic and polystyrene and weighs less than its pilot. The only power comes from the pilot pedalling furiously, but it went on to fly the English Channel and did so without using even a drop of fossil fuel.

The ability to build and operate machines like these is one of the things that separates humans from animals – that and the desire to do it in the first place. Some of them are useful, others are just a bit of fun, but the best ones are truly magnificent, and fascinating to discover.

1885
The first car, the Benz Patent Motorwagen, makes its first journey

1910
Fiat designs 'the Beast of Turin' to break the world land speed record

1911
The eight-wheeled Octoauto is created . . .

1923
The first Motoruota, a type of one-wheeled motorbike, is unveiled

1952
The American Boeing B-52 Stratofortress, the world's largest bomber, takes to the sky for the first time

1944
The Panzerkampfwagen VIII Maus is completed, the heaviest tank in the world

1890   **1900**   **1910**   **1920**   **1930**   **1940**   **1950**

1885   **1895**   **1905**   **1915**   **1925**   **1935**   **1945**

1912
. . . A six-wheeled Sextoauto joins it

The RMS Titanic sinks after hitting an iceberg

1927
The Bugatti Royale, the car built for kings, goes on sale

1936
First flight of Germany's LZ129 Hindenburg, the largest and longest flying machine in history

1937
The Hindenburg falls to the ground in flames

1947
The Spruce Goose, the largest ever seaplane, makes its first and only flight

1948
The McDonnell Goblin, one of the smallest aircraft, makes its first flight

TIMELINE

1960
The Hawker Siddeley Harrier 'Jump Jet' makes its first flight

1962
The tiny Peel P50 microcar is launched

The Ferrari 250 GTO, now the world's most valuable car, goes on sale

1964
First flight of the massively fast SR-71 spy plane

1971
Lunar rovers (or Moon buggies) are used as part of the Apollo missions to the Moon

1972
Launch of the USS Nimitz, the world's largest warship

1973
First appearance of Canada's Terex 33-19, the king of trucks

1983
The BD-5J, the world's smallest jet aircraft, appears in a James Bond film

2003
Concorde makes its final flight

2007
China's high-speed train service begins operating

2011
Stratolaunch Systems Corporation is formed to create an aeroplane designed to launch rockets into space

1960   **1970**   **1980**   **1990**   **2000**   **2010**   **2020**

55   **1965**   **1975**   **1985**   **1995**   **2005**   **2015**

1967
Saturn V rocket's first flight

1969
Maiden flght of Concorde, the Anglo-French supersonic airliner

1976
Kitty Hambleton becomes the fastest woman on earth while driving the SM1 Motivator

1979
The Gossamer Albatross becomes the first human-powered aircraft

Seawise Giant, the largest ship ever built, is launched to cross the English Channel

1989
Concorde flies right around the world

First flight of the Bell Boeing V-22 Osprey, the most expensive helicopter ever built

1995
The Bagger 293 is completed, the largest land vehicle on Earth

2008
Work begins on the Bloodhound LSR, an attempt to create the world's fastest car

2009
Eight vast tunnel boring machines begin digging London's new Elizabeth Line

Google launches its Waymo driverless car project

2020
The PAL-V Liberty flying car prepares for lift-off

MOTORWAGEN

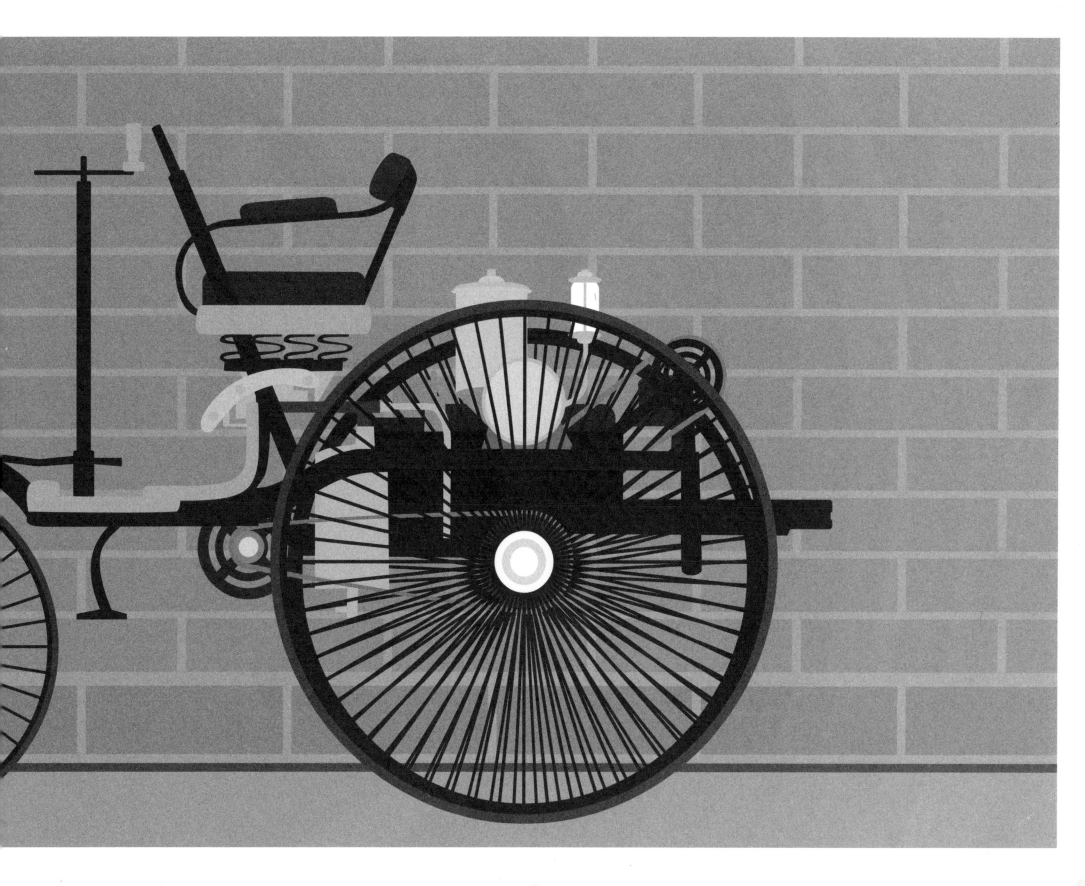

BENZ PATENT MOTORWAGEN

THE FIRST EVER AUTOMOBILE

» **Produced less than one horsepower**

» **Brakes made of wood**

» **Bystanders were terrified of the noise**

With more than a billion motor vehicles on the roads today, it is almost impossible to imagine a world without the motor car. However, the first one was only invented about **130** years ago. Before this most people had to walk everywhere, and almost everything they needed was carried on wagons pulled by horses.

The car's inventor, Karl Friedrich Benz, was a clever German engineer whose father was a train driver. Karl trained as a locksmith and was fascinated by machines of all sorts. Like many people were starting to do, he travelled around on a bicycle, but he could see that having everything else pulled by horses caused a lot of problems, especially in towns and cities.

Horses need feeding and watering, and on average each one produces around sixteen kilograms of manure and nearly ten litres of urine every single day. So in a big city like London or Berlin, with several hundred thousand working animals, the streets were always filthy and the smell was awful.

Karl was determined to find an alternative. Before long he had a company manufacturing industrial machines. These included a series of small engines, which were powered by a type of gas made from coal. The company was successful, and Karl employed two dozen people, but he never lost his love of bicycles or gave up his idea of inventing something to replace the horse.

In 1885 he began to construct what he called his Benz Patent Motorwagen. Being interested in bicycles, he chose tall, narrow wheels with wire spokes. These were much lighter than the heavy wooden wheels fitted to carts and carriages. He also designed a brand new engine, which was small but quite advanced for the time. It was located between the rear wheels, which were driven by a pair of chains.

The steering wheel wouldn't be invented for another decade, so Karl's car used a rod called a tiller, which worked a bit like a rudder on a boat.

The little engine produced less than one horsepower. Most family cars today are at least a hundred times more powerful, but this was more than enough for Karl's spindly three-wheeler, especially as it turned out to be quite difficult to drive. The steering wheel wouldn't be invented for another decade, so Karl's car used a rod called a tiller, which worked a bit like a rudder on a boat. Unfortunately,

while showing it to the people of his local town, Karl lost control of the tiller and smashed into a brick wall.

Luckily nobody was hurt, and after making a few repairs Karl decided to build a few more of them to sell. Sales were very slow to begin with, much like the car itself. Without any gears, drivers found it difficult to climb even quite small hills. Also the experience of rolling down a slope could be terrifying in a car with wooden brakes that didn't work very well.

Incredibly, Karl's company has survived. Today it's called Mercedes-Benz and is recognised all around the world.

But this all changed in 1888 when Karl's wife Bertha borrowed one to drive to her mother's house. This was **66 miles** away, much further than her husband had ever driven. Bertha took along their two teenage sons for company and hoped that the journey would be a good advertisement for the car. Along the way she suffered several breakdowns. Luckily she could fix the car herself, at one point using a hatpin to unblock a pipe. Bertha also thought of a simple way to improve the wooden brakes and stopped to ask a shoemaker to cover them in leather.

This worked surprisingly well and her successful trip persuaded several people living locally that her husband's clever machines were safe after all. Some were still scared by the noise the car made, but others liked the idea and before long Karl's company had sold twenty-five models, mostly in Germany and France. Other models followed, including a four-wheeler called the Velo, which competed in the world's first motor race. (It could do about **8 mph**, which is a good running speed for a boy or girl.) The company also produced the very first motorised trucks, one of which was later modified to become the world's first ever motor bus.

It didn't take long for other companies to copy Karl's idea, and before long nearly **4,000** of them were building cars of their own in lots of different countries. Not all of them did very well and most of them no longer exist, but, incredibly, Karl's company has survived. Today it's called Mercedes-Benz, and its badge (a three-pointed star, representing 'engines for land, air and water') is recognised all around the world.

FIAT

TIPO S76

FIAT TIPO S76

THE FIRST REALLY MONSTER ENGINE

» **Built to break the world land speed record**

» **Engine originally designed for a plane, not a car**

» **Makes a noise like you wouldn't believe!**

In the early days of motor racing the easiest way to get a car to go faster was to fit it with the largest engine possible. One of the biggest was squeezed under the bonnet of the 'Beast of Turin'. This was designed in 1910 to break the world land speed record, and named after the Italian city where it was built.

A modern Grand Prix car has a **1.6 litre** engine and a top speed of around **220 mph**. That's almost exactly twice as fast as the Beast's official top speed, although it has an engine which is about eighteen times larger at **28.5 litres**. And unlike Formula One cars, which have had up to sixteen cylinders, the Fiat has only four.

The Fiat would have the largest car engine on sale today even if it had only one cylinder instead of four.

These cylinders are absolute whoppers though and were originally designed to power an airship. Each one is more than seventy-five times larger than the smallest cylinder in an F1 engine. In fact, because each of them is so big (at **7.1 litres**) the Fiat would have the largest car engine on sale today even if it had only one cylinder instead of four.

The Tipo S76 was built at a time when leading manufacturers were competing against each other to produce the world's fastest car. Racing across a frozen lake in north America a Ford 999 managed just over **90 mph** with an engine of **18.1 litres**. In 1904 that was faster than anyone had ever driven. Five years later

Germany's Mercedes produced a challenger of its own, a car called the Blitzen Benz or 'lightning car'.

This had an even bigger engine than the Ford, at **21.5 litres**, and took the record up to **125 mph**, which was faster than even an aeroplane could manage at this time. Customers couldn't actually buy these terrifying machines, but manufacturers hoped that people would be impressed enough by the record-breakers to buy an ordinary car from the same factory.

The Fiat S76 was the first time anyone had attempted the record using an aircraft engine instead of a car one.

The Tipo S76 was Fiat's first attempt to do the same for Italy. It was by far the country's fastest ever car, but in official tests Pietro Bordino couldn't get it to go beyond **116 mph**. Another driver who was brave enough to try

it later on claimed to have driven faster than this on an ordinary Belgian road, but it was still not fast enough to claim the world record.

The Fiat S76 is interesting though because it was the first time anyone had attempted the record using an aircraft engine instead of a car one. When Fiat's next attempt managed to lift the record to **146 mph**, the idea caught on very quickly and, for almost forty years, every successful record attempt was done in a car powered by an aircraft engine.

The speeds rose higher and higher as the technology improved. For several years World War II put a stop to the record attempts, but then in 1947 Englishman John Cobb hit an astonishing **394.19 mph**.

Like Cobb's streamlined Railton Mobil Special, many of the fastest cars used engines from British aircraft engine manufacturers such as Napier and Rolls-Royce. The best of these was probably the Rolls-Royce R, which went on to break the world records for aircraft and boats as well as cars. It was later developed into the Merlin engine and powered several famous World War II aircraft, including the Hurricane, Spitfire and Lancaster bomber.

The most bizarre, however, was the American Triplex Special. As the name suggests this didn't use one aircraft engine or even two but three. Each of its huge Liberty V12s was almost as big as the Fiat's entire engine, giving the car a total of eighty-one litres and no fewer than thirty-six cylinders. That's as many cylinders as half a dozen Formula One cars today, and it was enough for the car to hold the record for a few months. Unfortunately it was so scary and dangerous that the driver refused to drive it a second time. When another driver was persuaded to take his place, the Triplex crashed, killing both him and a watching cameraman.

REEVES

OCTOAUTO

OCTOAUTO

MILTON'S WACKY EIGHT-WHEELER

» **Inventor promised a smoother ride**

» **It was expensive though, and too long to park**

» **The next version had only six wheels**

Most cars have four wheels, but over the years designers and engineers have experimented with two-, three-, five-, six- and even eight-wheeled versions.

The strangest was created by an inventor called Milton Reeves, an early pioneer of the American automobile industry. He and his brother Marshall were responsible for more than a hundred inventions, including a strange bus with wheels nearly two metres

in diameter and several devices for use in factories and on farms.

Reeves began building an eight-wheeled car, which he called the Octoauto, in 1911. The bodywork was like most others at the time but with four axles and eight wheels it looked very strange indeed. Because it was more than six metres long it was also very hard to manoeuvre. Only two of the eight wheels steered and it was almost impossible to park anywhere in a town or city. It was very expensive as well, and costing more than five times as much as a Ford Model T, the world's best-selling car.

> ## *Only two of the eight wheels steered and it was almost impossible to park anywhere in a town or city.*

Reeves was convinced it was a good idea though, and that his car offered a smoother ride than its rivals. He also claimed it suffered fewer punctures despite having twice as many tyres. Sadly for him most drivers were happy with only four wheels, and it soon became clear that no one was interested in buying one of his eight-wheelers. Reeves refused to give up, however, and decided that if eight

wheels were too many then his customers might like six.

He called his next car the Sextoauto and fitted it with three axles instead of four. Unfortunately he also put the price up. Now his car cost **$5,000** – equivalent to ten Ford Model Ts – and once again no one was interested in buying it.

After this Reeves decided he'd had enough. His other inventions had made him and his brother rich. Their factory employed more than a thousand people, and he decided not to build any more cars. Today a car as rare as the Octoauto or the Sextoauto would be quite valuable, but unfortunately neither of them has survived.

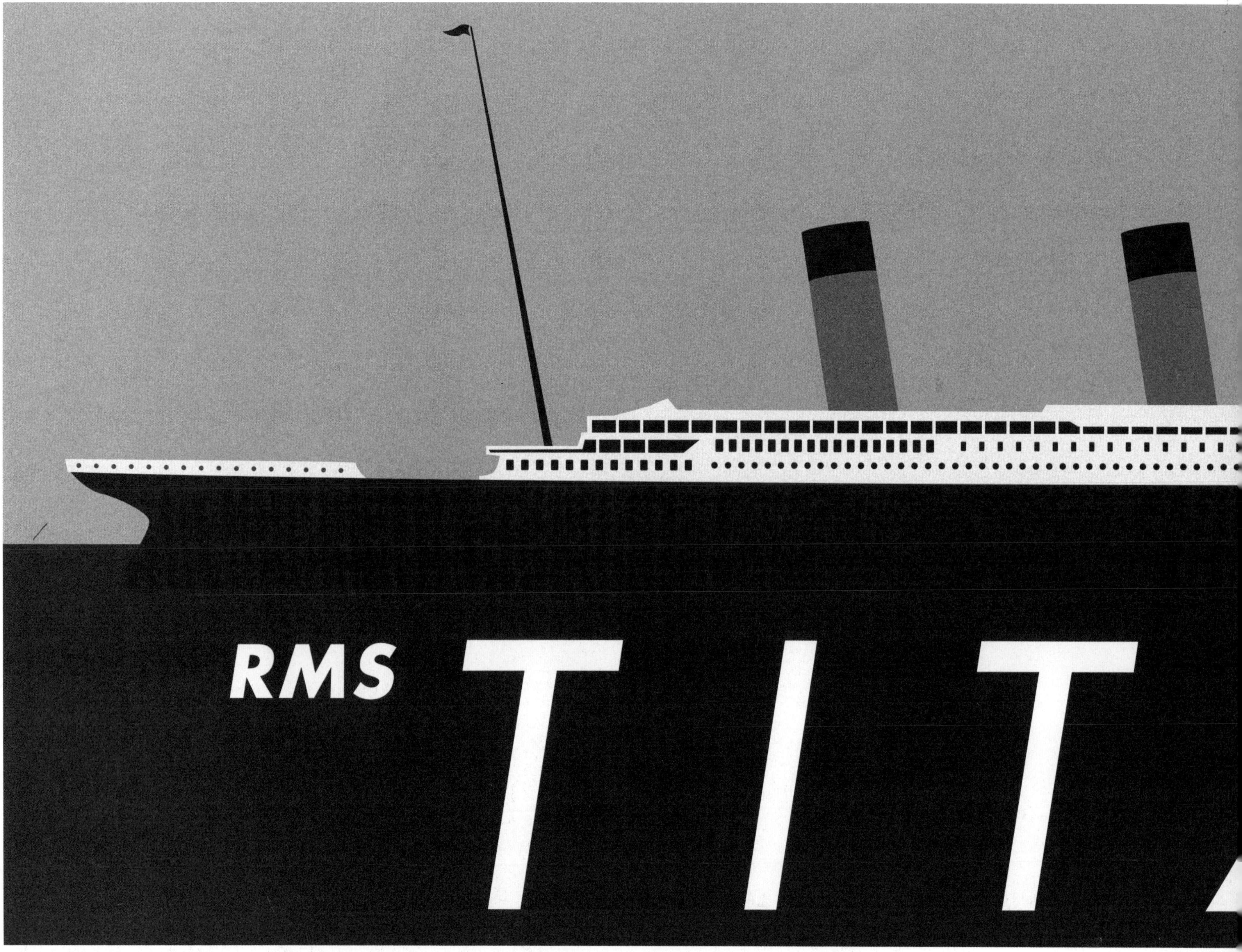
RMS
TIT

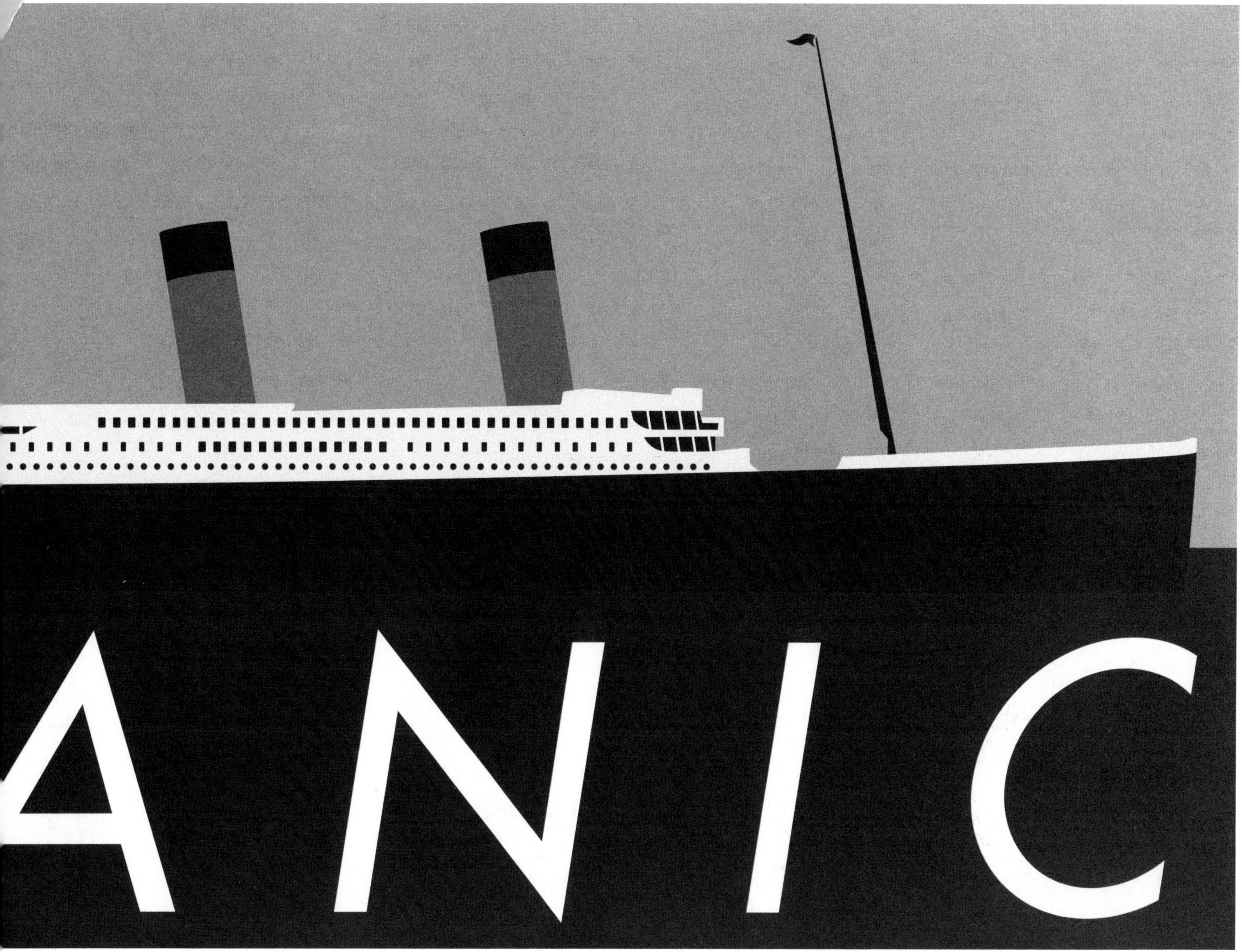
A N I C

RMS TITANIC

THE TRAGIC *TITANIC*

» **The world's biggest ship when launched**

» **The owners called it unsinkable**

» **But it sank on its first ever voyage**

Fewer than **3,400** people ever travelled on it, and it made only one voyage, but after more than a hundred years it is still the most famous ship in history.

In 1912 it was the largest vessel afloat. *Titanic*'s combination of size, advanced design and new technology meant that many people thought it would be impossible for the ship to sink. Unfortunately this turned out not to be true. Just before midnight on 14 April that year, *Titanic* struck an iceberg far out in the Atlantic Ocean. She sank to a depth of more than two miles and more than 1,500 passengers and crew were killed.

The tragedy was not the worst ever shipping disaster. As many as 9,400 people are thought to have died when the *Wilhelm Gustloff* sank in 1945, and more recently nearly

4,400 people drowned after a ferry in the Philippines collided with an oil tanker. But there has always been something special about the *Titanic* which captured the public's imagination. Interest in it has never gone away and today even small items associated with the ship, like a menu or a piece of cutlery, are enormously valuable.

She was certainly a magnificent machine. Just over **269 metres** long and powered by two giant steam engines, each day the **29** boilers consumed **600 tonnes** of coal and produced a horrifying **100 tonnes** of ash (this

She was just over 269 metres long and the main anchor was so heavy it took twenty horses just to move it!

was thrown overboard). The main anchor was so heavy it took twenty horses just to move it, and the metal panels that made up the hull were held together by more than three million rivets.

Tickets for its first transatlantic voyage cost as little as **$30** but the best suites were **145** times more expensive. Passengers booking suites could enjoy all the ship's luxury facilities, which included a gym, swimming pool and squash court, several libraries, and a restaurant modelled on the fabulous Ritz Hotel in London.

To accommodate all this the *Titanic* was big…but unfortunately the iceberg was even bigger. It is now thought to have been at least **100,000** years old and to have drifted down from Greenland. Scientists calculate that it must have been **500 metres** long and weighed several million tonnes. Icebergs mostly lie hidden beneath the water but although

Because the sea was so deep it took more than seventy years to find the wreck of the Titanic.

the bit poking above the waves would still have been huge no one saw this one until it was too late.

As the ship began to sink a member of the crew managed to send a distress signal by radio and soon another liner called the *Carpathia* arrived. Unfortunately it arrived too late for many of the victims. The *Titanic* had more lifeboats than most liners at the time, but there weren't enough for everyone on board. No one could survive for long floating in the near-freezing water of the north Atlantic. Most of those who couldn't clamber into a lifeboat quickly drowned. Among the 1,517 dead were the ship's captain Edward Smith and its designer Thomas Andrews.

Because the sea was so deep it took more than seventy years to find the wreck of the *Titanic*, and hundreds of bodies have never been recovered. Interestingly, after all this time, it is still the second largest passenger ship on the sea floor. It is beaten only by its sister ship, the *Britannic*, which sank five years later with the loss of another thirty lives.

MOTORUOTA
MONOWHEEL

MOTORUOTA MONOWHEEL

SITTING IN A SINGLE WHEEL

» **The driver can't see where he's going**

» **There's nowhere to put any luggage**

» **And it's too big to fit in anyone's garage**

Today it's possible to buy three-wheeled motorbikes, with the extra wheel at the front or at the back, but in the 1920s two Italians built several which had only one. Giuseppe Govetosa and Davide Cislaghi's wheels were so big that the rider sat inside rather than on top, like a clown riding a circus unicycle.

Small but powerful engines made these machines as fast as conventional motorbikes of the time, and one of them could do nearly **100 mph**. Unfortunately having only one wheel caused the Italians many difficulties and it's not hard to see why their idea never caught on.

Making the wheel large enough for someone to sit inside it meant the Motoruota was taller than most cars. It couldn't be stored in a shed or a garage like a normal motorbike, and visibility was a serious problem. The wheel rim blocked the rider's view of the road ahead, and if he leaned out to the left or right to see where he was going the machine would automatically turn in that direction or become unbalanced and fall over.

The Motoruota was reasonably stable as long as it was moving along but when the rider stopped at a junction or at a set of traffic lights he had to stick out his legs and put his feet on the ground. Even then the machine might topple on to its side because it was so tall and heavy. Having one wheel meant the machine was also more likely to skid on a wet or icy road than a bike with two or three wheels.

There was also a risk with some designs that if the driver accelerated suddenly or if he braked sharply he would be sent spinning round like a hamster in an exercise wheel. Engineers call this 'gerbiling', which sounds quite funny but could be highly dangerous.

The Motoruota's biggest problem, though, was that almost no one could see the point of buying one. It was much bigger than a motorbike but it could still carry only one person. There was nowhere for any luggage and if somebody couldn't afford a car he or she was far better off with an ordinary motorbike, which cost less to buy and was far more practical.

Because of this it's unlikely that the Motoruota ever made any money for its inventor, and the few that were built have now disappeared. That hasn't stopped other inventors trying out similar ideas, however. Some of these rely on pedal-power, including a Chinese one which looks quite fun, and at least one is electric. The most terrifying examples have been fitted with huge aircraft-like propellers, which would be incredibly dangerous for any pedestrians walking nearby. Like the Motoruota, none of these have survived, which is probably just as well.

BUGATTI R

OYALE

BUGATTI TYPE 41 'ROYALE'

A CAR BUILT FOR KINGS

» **Each one cost more than three Rolls-Royces**

» **Only royalty could buy them**

» **The bonnet mascot is solid silver**

With a top speed of more than **260 mph** the Bugatti Chiron is one of the fastest and most powerful cars ever made, but ninety years ago one of its ancestors was something *really* special.

The earlier Bugatti Type 41 was designed to be larger and more luxurious than any car ever built. In the 1920s it was nicknamed the 'Royale' and was also much more expensive than any other car, with a price tag of just over £10,000. This may not sound like much by modern standards, but in 1927 it was enough to buy at least three top-of-the-range Rolls-Royce Phantoms. This was at a time when the average British worker earned only **£5** a week, and an entire three-bedroom house cost less than **£300**.

The French car manufacturer was already famous for its elegant and technologically advanced cars. Its little

Type 35 was the most successful racing car in the world and won more than a thousand races, but with the Type 41 the company owner, Ettore Bugatti, wanted to create something entirely different.

Where the Type 35 was small and nimble, the Type 41 was the longest car on the road. (At **6.4 metres** only a few modern stretch limos are longer.) Where the Type 35 was light and delicate the Type 41 tipped the scales at more than three tonnes, making it one of the heaviest cars ever sold. This meant the engine had to be enormous too, and it certainly was. The Chiron has an eight-litre engine, which is huge, but the Type 41 easily beats it at **12.7 litres**. That's so big that the volume of each of its eight cylinders is larger than the entire engine of the earlier Type 40 model. In fact, the engine is exactly a thousand times larger than

the smallest one Bugatti designed so perhaps it's not surprising that the same engines were later used to power railway locomotives.

Naturally these incredible, extravagant cars were also highly luxurious. The interiors were created by skilled French craftsmen using embroidered silk, handworked metal and polished wood from some of the world's rarest trees. Even the bonnet mascot was made of solid silver, a striking model of an African elephant rearing up on its hind legs. The other special thing about the Royale is that none of them were the same as each other. The cars were all designed with completely different body styles, and had different interiors, so that rich owners would never suffer the embarrassment of meeting someone else who had a similar car.

He decided that the Type 41 would only be sold to royalty.

Ettore insisted that, as this was his finest creation so far, only the finest people would be allowed to buy it. He decided that the Type 41 would only be sold to royalty. He planned to build twenty-five of them (the world had many more kings and queens than it has today), but perhaps it was too expensive even for them. In the end the factory built just six Royales. Only three were sold, and none of them to royalty.

King Alfonso of Spain wanted to buy one, but had to flee his country when the Spanish people threatened a revolution. King Zog of Albania wanted one too, but Ettore refused to sell it to him, saying he didn't like the king's table manners. In fact only King Carol of Romania seems to have come close to buying one, but then another revolution meant he lost his throne as well before he had a chance to drive it.

The first of these amazing cars was sadly destroyed in 1931 when Ettore Bugatti fell asleep at the wheel and crashed. Another somehow ended up on a scrap heap in New York before being rescued and restored by a man who paid only a few hundred dollars for the wreck. And a third was hidden in a Paris sewer to save it from the German army when France was invaded in 1940.

Fortunately it was rescued from the sewer when the war ended and today five of the six survivors are on display in museums in France, Germany and America. Strangely no one knows who owns the sixth one, or where it is. When he died in 1947 Ettore Bugatti gave two of the unsold cars to his daughter L'Ebé who swapped them for a pair of large American refrigerators. One ended up in a museum in California, but the whereabouts of the second is still a multi-million-dollar mystery . . .

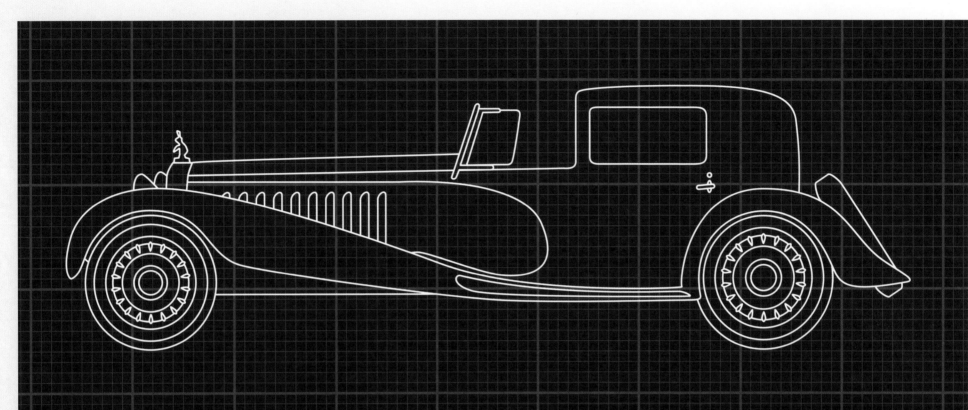

BUGATTI TYPE 41 'ROYALE'

LENGTH: 6.4 metres
WHEELBASE: 4.3 metres
WIDTH: 2.1 metres
WEIGHT: 3,175 kilograms
ENGINE: 12.76 litres,
8 cylinders

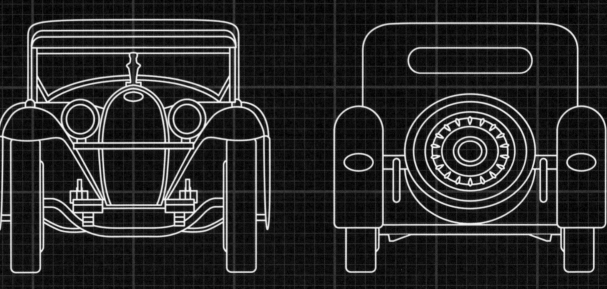

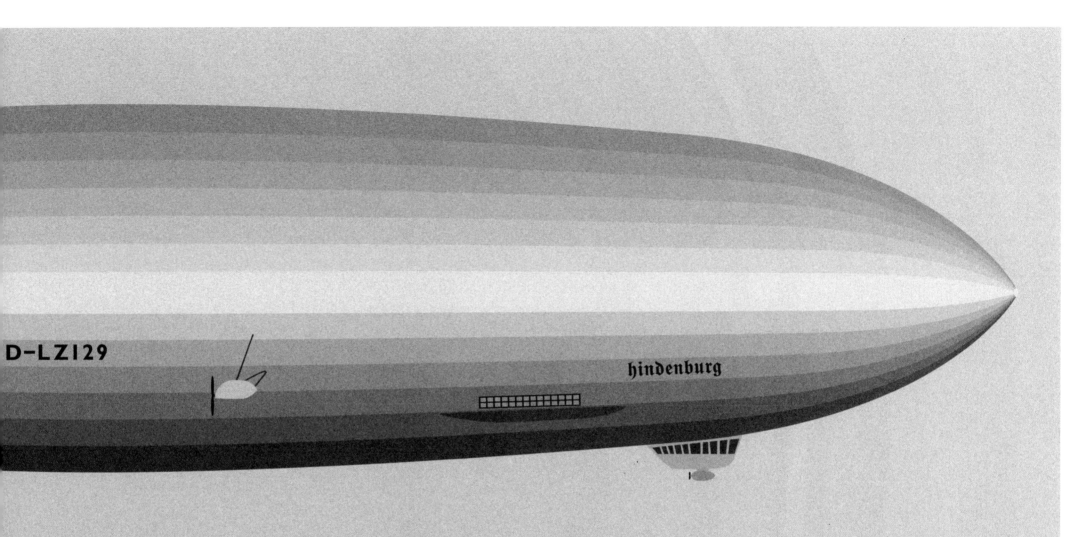

D-LZ129

hindenburg

LZ129
HINDENBURG

LZ129 HINDENBURG

GERMANY'S FLYING GIANT

» **The largest flying machine ever built**

» **It was longer than ten tennis courts**

» **When it caught fire it was destroyed in just half a minute**

There are many different ways to measure how big an aircraft is. The futuristic Stratolaunch (see page 164) is easily the widest with a wingspan of **117 metres**, but it's not as long as a Boeing 747-8 airliner. The Antonov An-225 is longer than the Boeing, and when fully loaded it weighs **640 tonnes**, which is more than **100** African elephants. It once carried a space shuttle on its roof, the largest single cargo ever flown, and inside there's enough room to transport an entire submarine.

But even at **88.4 metres** the six-engined Antonov looks tiny compared with Germany's LZ129 *Hindenburg*. This first flew in 1936, more than eighty years ago, and it still holds the record as the largest and longest flying machine ever built. Stretching **245 metres** from one end to the other, it was almost five times as long as than an Olympic swimming pool.

Gigantic airships were popular in the 1930s, and this was easily the most gigantic. None of them was fast but the

Hindenburg was incredibly luxurious and gave passengers the chance to fly much longer distances than an ordinary aeroplane could manage at the time.

In those days aeroplanes couldn't travel more than a few hundred miles without stopping to refuel. Flying from Europe to Australia now takes less than a day, but in the 1930s a flight could last eleven days and require no fewer than twenty-four refuelling stops along the way.

Airships could make much longer flights because they were lighter than air. Millions of litres of gas kept them airborne so the engines were needed only to manoeuvre the airship and to send it in the right direction. Initially the engineers were planning to fit ten to the *Hindenburg*, but they found that four were enough, each one powering a huge **5.7 metre** propeller. This meant the airship would be quieter and use less fuel than an aeroplane and could travel much, much further.

Soon after the *Hindenburg* was completed, the Zeppelin company which owned it began operating flights from Frankfurt in Germany to the United States. Passenger aircraft weren't yet able to cross the Atlantic and so the airship offered the only alternative to making the journey by ship. Flying at **85 mph**, it took two and a half days to cover the distance a modern jet will manage in a few hours, but even the fastest ocean liner took five days. Some took ten or more, and many rich customers preferred to pay extra to save time by flying.

The *Hindenburg* was also far more luxurious than an aeroplane, with a shower and proper bedrooms for its seventy-two passengers. There was wonderful food, a cocktail bar and comfortable lounge areas. There was even a dance floor with a grand piano made from special lightweight metal, and on the *Hindenburg*'s first transatlantic flight the Pope gave permission for a priest to hold a Catholic service high above the ocean.

The views from the large windows were spectacular, but perhaps the most surprising thing was a special room set aside for smoking. Passengers were allowed to do this even though the airship contained **20,000,000 litres** of hydrogen gas. This is even more flammable than petrol and even the tiniest spark could cause a massive explosion which would have been catastrophic.

The gas was held in sixteen vast balloon-like bags, each one as large as several houses. Bags in older airships were made using the intestines of several hundred thousand cattle. The *Hindenburg* claimed to be more advanced, and used a special cotton fabric which was impregnated with chemicals to reduce the possibility of leaks.

Unfortunately small leaks were impossible to avoid and in May 1937 disaster struck as the *Hindenburg* arrived at its landing site in the American state of New Jersey. Thousands of spectators and four film crews had gathered to see the magnificent machine manoeuvring overhead, but their cheers turned to screams when flames were spotted rippling along its silvery length.

In seconds the entire airship was ablaze and came crashing to the ground. Some of the passengers managed, somehow, to leap to safety, but thirteen were killed in the tragedy, together with twenty-two members of the crew. Film of the disaster was shown around the world and this convinced travellers that airships were no longer safe. As airliners improved to make longer and longer journeys, the public lost interest in these fabulous giants of the skies.

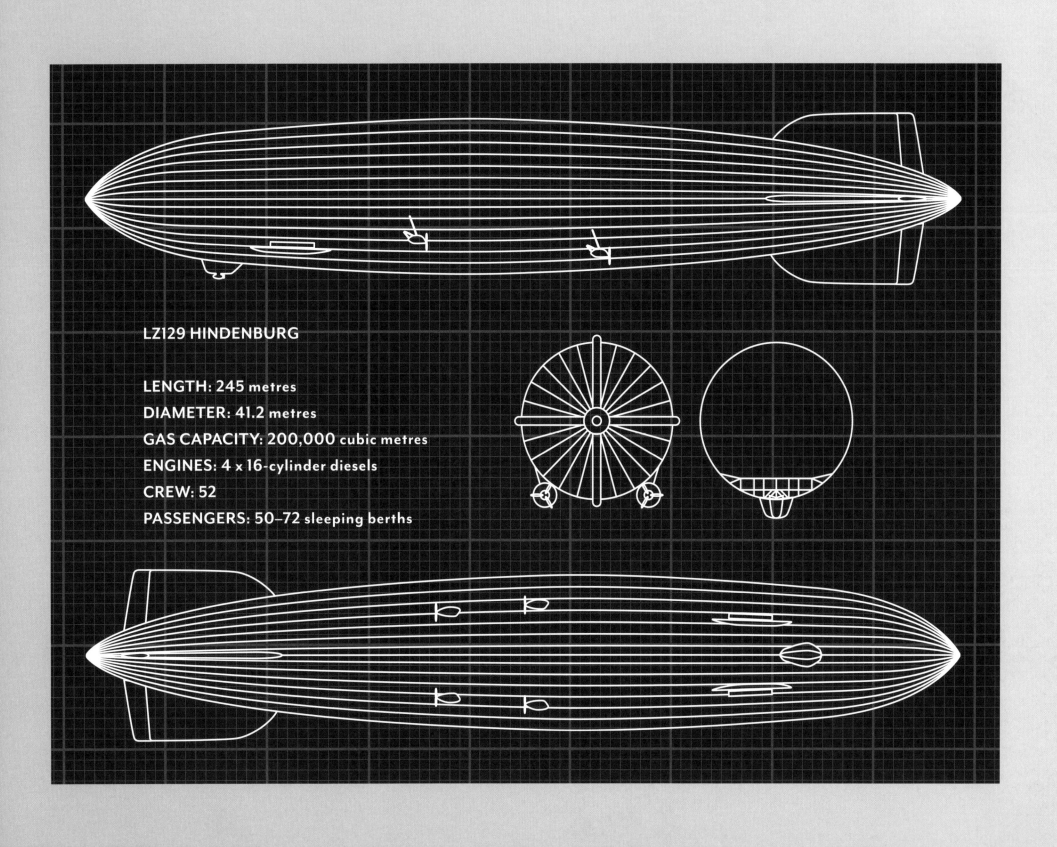

LZ129 HINDENBURG

LENGTH: 245 metres

DIAMETER: 41.2 metres

GAS CAPACITY: 200,000 cubic metres

ENGINES: 4 x 16-cylinder diesels

CREW: 52

PASSENGERS: 50–72 sleeping berths

PANZERKAMPFWAGEN
VIII

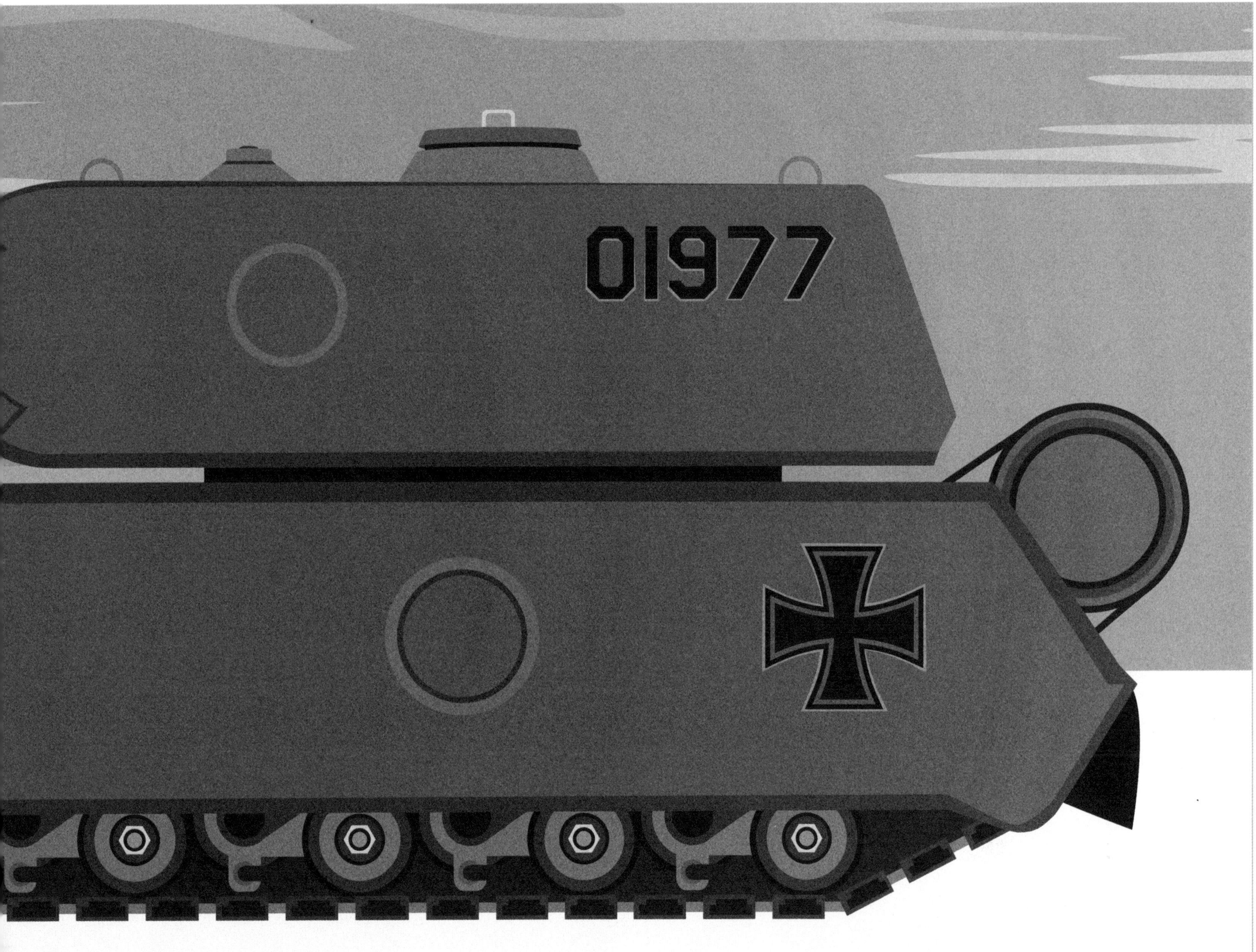
01977

PANZERKAMPFWAGEN VIII

THE HEAVIEST TANK EVER BUILT

- » Six times heavier than an ordinary tank
- » Could fire a shell more than two miles
- » . . . But could still only do twelve miles an hour

The largest tank ever built was too heavy for most bridges so was designed to trundle along the riverbed whenever it needed to cross a river.

Nicknamed the *Maus* or Mouse, Germany's Panzerkampfwagen VIII was the brainchild of a brilliant engineer called Ferdinand Porsche. He later became famous for building sports cars, but during World War II he designed several terrifying weapons including tanks and flying bombs.

His *Maus* weighed **188 tonnes**, the same as six or seven ordinary German tanks. It was not only larger than them but had incredibly thick armour plating, more than twenty centimetres in places. This protected the six-man crew and explains why it had to be designed to wade through deep water. Even the most modern bridge at the time would probably have collapsed under its weight.

44

Its main gun was equally enormous and could fire **28kg** shells more than two miles. One of them could punch a hole in any building and would completely destroy an enemy tank. Its other weapons included a powerful machine gun and a special cannon for firing upwards at aeroplanes.

Normal engines were not powerful enough at this time to propel anything this heavy, so Porsche developed a hybrid system that worked like a modern Toyota Prius. Inside the tank's body a huge **44 litre** V12 engine from a Messerschmitt bomber powered an electric generator. Electricity from this was used to drive two massive caterpillar tracks, each more than a metre wide. The tank was still very slow and so Porsche tried

The Maus weighed 188 tonnes, the same as six or seven ordinary German tanks.

a more powerful, supercharged engine but, even with **1,200 horsepower**, the top speed of the *Maus* was still only **12 mph**. That doesn't sound like much, although it's hard to think of anything that could have stopped it once it started moving.

The *Maus* would have been deadly but fortunately it was never used in battle because the Germans built only two of them before losing the war. The first was destroyed in a huge explosion, and the second was captured by the Russian army. They took it back to Moscow, which took weeks, and it now lives in a special museum.

HUGHES
HERCULES H-4

HERCULES H-4

HISTORY'S LARGEST SEAPLANE

» **Large enough to carry 750 soldiers at a time**

» **Made of wood, not metal**

» **. . . But it flew only once, and covered barely a mile**

When the world's richest inventor set out to build the world's biggest aeroplane, the result was a wooden giant that became known as the Spruce Goose.

Billionaire pilot Howard Hughes chose wood because during World War II it was almost impossible to find enough of the right kind of metal. His design was for a type of aircraft called a flying boat, meaning one that can take off and land on water. Able to fly all the way to Britain without stopping to refuel, his H-4 Hercules was large enough to carry **750** fully armed soldiers or two **38-tonne** Sherman tanks.

In 1942, as part of its plan to support troops fighting in Europe, the American government ordered three of these gigantic aircraft. Thousands of men and weapons were being sent across the Atlantic by sea at this time, but the ships they travelled in were slow and were often sunk by German submarines. Transporting everything by air sounded safer, and with its eight powerful engines the **250 mph** Spruce Goose would be able to make the journey in a few hours instead of the ten or more days it took a ship.

The fuselage and wings were constructed using thin layers of wood and a glue-like stuff called Duramold. This made them light and very strong, but work on the prototype was slow. Also, because it was so large, the aircraft had to be transported in massive sections to its launch site. The sections travelled by road across California before being fitted together so that the finished machine could be towed out to sea.

Building any new aircraft takes a long time but, as you can imagine, doing it this way took even longer. In fact, it took so long that by the time the prototype was finished and ready to fly the war was over. Now the government didn't want to pay for any more aircraft, and with so many airfields and runways left over from the war no one needed aeroplanes that could take off from the water.

The H-4 Hercules was large enough to carry 750 fully armed soldiers

Hughes was furious about this and threatened to leave America forever. Determined to prove that his aeroplane worked, he took the controls for what turned out to be its first and only flight. With a handful of lucky passengers, the graceful giant flew just over a mile before landing softly back on the sea. The Spruce Goose reached a height of only twenty-one metres, but Hughes had made his point: it worked and looked beautiful. Seventy years on, his fabulous creation is still the largest flying boat ever built, and it's become a hugely popular museum exhibit.

MCDONNELL
GOBLIN

MCDONNELL GOBLIN

A PLANE THE SIZE OF A BOMB

» **Designed to be carried inside a bomber**

» **No wheels because it was never meant to land**

» **Only two were built**

The McDonnell XF-85 Goblin was so small it could be carried inside the body of another aeroplane.

In the 1940s and 1950s most bombers were large, slow and heavy. This made them easy targets for other aircraft, and if they flew long distances it was often impossible for defending fighters to accompany them all the way. One solution to this problem was for the bomber to carry its own tiny fighter jet on board, one which could be sent to attack any hostile aircraft the bomber encountered during a mission.

During the Cold War between Russia and America, nuclear bombers grew larger and larger. The largest was the American Convair B-36, which could fly **10,000 miles** and carry almost forty tonnes of bombs in four separate compartments. But even with ten engines (and huge **5.8 metre** propellers) the Convair's top speed was only **435 mph**.

The Goblin was designed to be small enough to be hidden inside one of the bomb bays.

This put it at risk from attack from much faster jet fighters, so the Goblin was designed to be small enough to be hidden inside one of the bomb bays. If a hostile jet was spotted the Goblin could be quickly lowered using a device called a trapeze and sent into action. Afterwards the pilot would return to the trapeze, hook the Goblin on to it and be winched back on board.

Unfortunately, like a sign of trouble to come, the first Goblin was dropped by a crane before it had flown even

once. It was so badly damaged a second one had to be built. This was fast and easy to fly, but the pilot found it impossible to hook back up to the trapeze. This meant he had to land it in the normal way but because the Goblin wasn't designed to do this it didn't have any wheels. The pilot was lucky enough to survive what's called a 'belly landing' but now the second Goblin was badly damaged too.

Hearing this, the air force quickly lost interest in the project. Apart from anything else, better missile technology was beginning to make it possible to shoot down these old bombers without using fighters. Clearly a whole new type of bomber was needed, one that could fly higher and faster using jet engines. Soon the idea of anyone carrying an aeroplane inside an aeroplane sounded weird and old-fashioned, and the poor little Goblin was quickly forgotten.

BOEING

B - 52

BOEING B-52

THE BIGGEST EVER BOMBER

» **Eight engines instead of four**

» **Burns 11,000 litres of fuel an hour**

» **Carries 30 tonnes of bombs on a single mission**

Everything about the American Boeing B-52 Stratofortress is enormous. The gigantic wings stretch fifty-six metres from tip to tip, making it wider than a football pitch and giving them the same surface area as one and a half tennis courts. Its body is longer than that of most airliners, most of which have only two or four engines where the B-52 has eight.

Standing on the runway, it's also seriously tall. Taller than

a double-decker bus. Taller than a double-decker parked on top of *another* double-decker. In fact, it's as tall as one double-decker parked on top of another double-decker with a car parked on top of that.

The engines burn more than **11,000 litres** of fuel an hour but thanks to monster fuel tanks a B-52 can fly nearly **9,000 miles** without stopping. It can do this while carrying **30 tonnes** of bombs, or about the same as three of Britain's famous Avro Vulcans. As the world's first true long-range bomber it has been engineered to fly more than nine miles above the ground, or nearly twice as high as Mount Everest. This means most of America's enemies wouldn't even see it coming, let alone be able to shoot it down.

The B-52 has carried just about everything from nuclear bombs to laser-guided cruise missiles, pilotless drones and even spare parts for the Space Shuttle.

But perhaps the most incredible thing about B-52s is that they're still flying today, more than **65** years after the first test flight. The US air force expects to them to stay on active duty for at least another two decades, by which time some of them will be more than eighty years old! In fact the B-52 is already so old that the first ones were designed to have old-fashioned propellers. When the air force suddenly changed its mind and announced it wanted jets instead, Boeing's engineers spent a frantic weekend working to produce what we see here.

The B-52 has carried just about everything from nuclear bombs to laser-guided cruise missiles, pilotless drones and even spare parts for the Space Shuttle. As one of America's favourite planes, it's also broken numerous speed and distance records. In 1957, for example, three of them flying in formation became the first jets ever to fly non-stop around the world. Covering an amazing **24,325 miles** took them less than two days, thereby slashing the existing record in half.

It was an extraordinary achievement, but it had a serious purpose too, which was to demonstrate that America could send its deadliest thermonuclear weapons anywhere in the world. Also known as hydrogen bombs, thermonuclear weapons are far more destructive than the atomic bombs dropped on Japan to end World War II. Those killed a horrifying 210,000 people, but they were small compared with later bombs, which can be up to **3,000** times as powerful.

Today these giants of the sky rarely carry such weapons, but they are still truly awesome machines. Huge, brutish, even ugly, many of those flying with the 96th Bomb Squadron have ferocious nicknames painted on their noses, like *The Grim Reaper*, *Apocalypse* and *The Devil's Own*.

With most of the aeroplane's vast interior taken up by weapons and fuel, conditions on board are horribly cramped for the crew of five. They liken the experience of climbing up the ladder from the hatch in its belly to boarding a submarine, and it's not hard to see why.

For one thing, only the pilot and aircraft commander have windows to see outside. The navigator, radar navigator and weapon systems officer spend their time in darkness. (For a while there was another member of the crew too, a tail gunner sitting alone nearly fifty metres away at the far end, but this job disappeared a few year ago.) A single mission can involve being airborne for **35 hours** or more – that's two days and a night – and the ladder is the only place where a person can actually stand up. Knowing this, it's hard to see how they cope, but as a crew member once put it, 'This aeroplane wasn't designed for people. It was designed for bombs.'

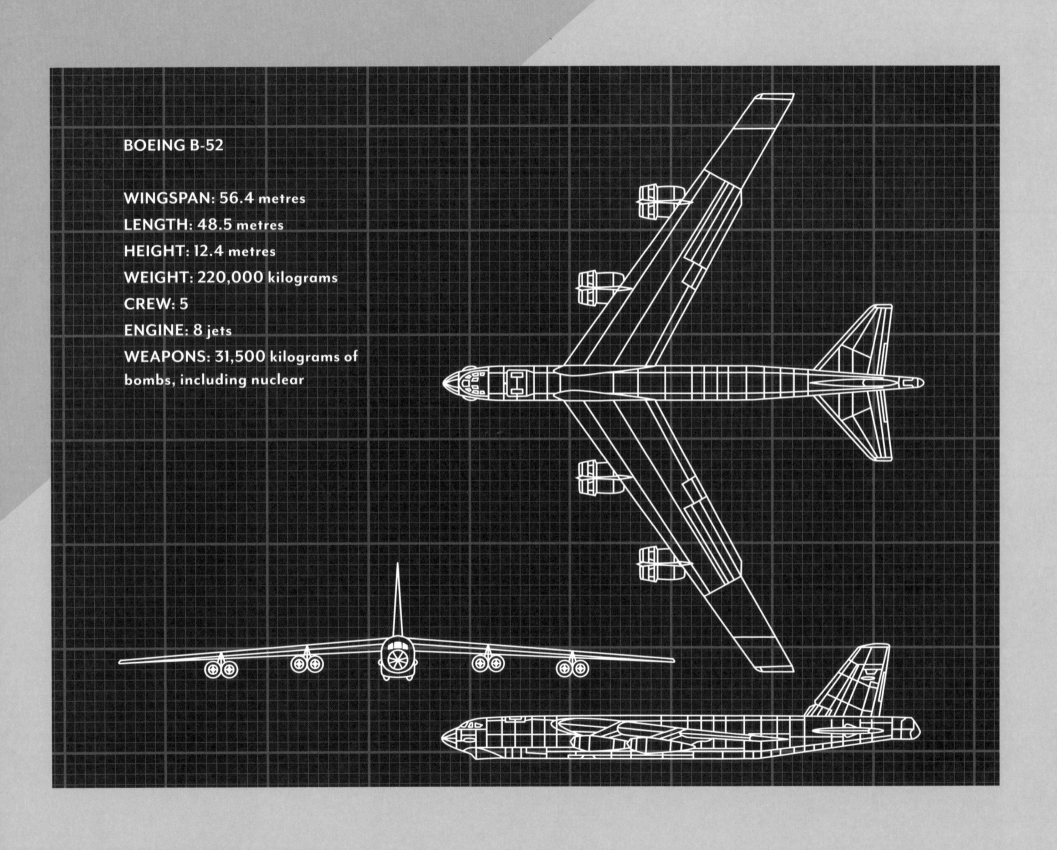

BOEING B-52

WINGSPAN: 56.4 metres
LENGTH: 48.5 metres
HEIGHT: 12.4 metres
WEIGHT: 220,000 kilograms
CREW: 5
ENGINE: 8 jets
WEAPONS: 31,500 kilograms of
bombs, including nuclear

74

XV708

HAWKER SIDDELEY
HARRIER

HAWKER SIDDELEY HARRIER

THE PLANE THAT COULD JUMP

» Takes off vertically

» Flies backwards

» It can even hover

Sir Sydney Camm was one of the most brilliant aircraft designers of the twentieth century. He created dozens of outstanding machines, beginning with biplanes in the 1920s and finishing with the astonishing Harrier which was still flying with British and American air forces ninety years later.

The Harrier was known as the 'Jump Jet' because unlike conventional fighters it could take off vertically. This made it perfect for military operations in areas where it wasn't possible to build or defend a normal runway. Because it could take off and land in a much smaller space than other fighters, the Harrier was fantastic for jungle and mountain warfare. It could also operate from ships which were smaller and much less expensive than aircraft carriers.

In wartime a country's airfields and military bases become important targets for its enemies. Each side uses bombs, mines, missiles and rockets to try to destroy the other side's aircraft and runways. Even if the aircraft themselves aren't damaged in this way, pilots can't take off if the surface of a runway is full of bomb craters and unexploded bombs.

Aircraft designers and engineers around the world had spent years and millions of pounds trying to find a way to make aircraft which could take off vertically.

This is where the Harrier really scored points. Because it could be hidden miles away from the air base (in a forest clearing, for example, or beneath camouflage netting in a remote desert area) the pilot could wait until the right moment to lift off and strike at an unsuspecting enemy. In this way Harriers could operate from a position close to the enemy, making it possible to launch rapid, surprise attacks.

Aircraft designers and engineers around the world had spent years and millions of pounds trying to find a way to make aircraft which could take off vertically. Helicopters can do it but most are too slow to be used in combat. Various experimental designs were tried in different countries but they didn't work or were too complicated to be reliable and were quickly scrapped.

Sir Sydney stuck with the idea and by 1960 he'd managed to build a prototype which could take off vertically and fly horizontally.

Sir Sydney stuck with the idea and by 1960 he'd managed to build a prototype which could take off vertically and fly horizontally. It used something called vectored thrust, an ingenious system of swivelling nozzles attached to the sides of the engine. If the pilot angles the nozzles backwards the aircraft flies forward like a normal jet. If they point towards the ground the power from the engine is also directed downwards, enabling the aircraft to lift into the air.

By manipulating the nozzles in this way, the pilot could take off from a standstill instead of needing a long runway to build up speed. Once airborne the Harrier could hover, dip its nose and even fly backwards. This extraordinary manoeuvrability made the Harrier a formidable fighting machine, as well as one of the stars at air shows, where pilots performed a sort of aerial ballet, to the delight of spectators from around the world.

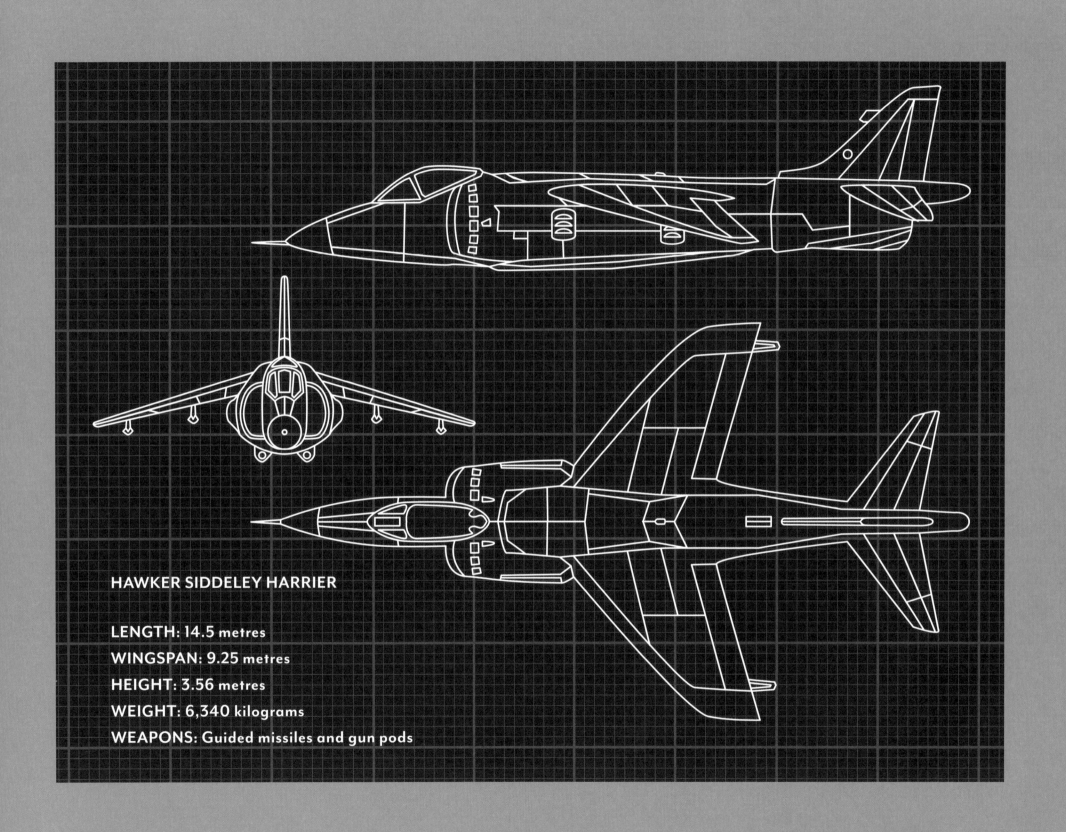

HAWKER SIDDELEY HARRIER

LENGTH: 14.5 metres

WINGSPAN: 9.25 metres

HEIGHT: 3.56 metres

WEIGHT: 6,340 kilograms

WEAPONS: Guided missiles and gun pods

PEEL P 50

PEEL P50

A CAR SO SMALL YOU CAN LIFT IT UP

» **Room for one and a bag of shopping**

» **One headlamp, and only three wheels**

» **Powered by a moped engine**

A shortage of money and raw materials after World War II meant that for several years ordinary cars were difficult to build and far too expensive for many motorists to buy.

A solution arrived in the shape of the micro- or bubble car, and before long dozens of manufacturers in Europe and America were producing tiny cars, jeeps and vans which people could afford to buy and run. Some were more imaginative than others, a few were surprisingly fast, and today the best are highly collectible and so quite valuable.

One of these is a three-wheeler called the Peel P50. It was built on the Isle of Man, which lies between England and Ireland. In 1962 a new one cost just **£199**, which was about a third of the price of a Mini. Exactly a metre tall, **99 centimetres** wide and just **134 centimetres** long, it's still the smallest production car ever produced.

Inside it has room for only one person and a bag of shopping, with a single door on the left-hand side and one headlamp instead of two. There's no reverse gear either, meaning the driver has to get out of the car and use a handle at the back to lift it up and turn it around. Luckily it doesn't weigh much so this isn't hard to do.

Inside it has room for only one person and a bag of shopping.

The tiny car also has a tiny engine, from a motorscooter. With only **49 cc**, it has a top speed of **38 mph**, but according to the manufacturer it was capable of doing **100 miles** on a single gallon of fuel, making it one of the most economical cars of all time.

Despite this the company managed to sell fewer than fifty P50s before going out of business. The little car was more or less forgotten until, years later, television presenter Jeremy Clarkson was filmed driving a blue one into a lift and around the offices of the BBC. After this more people became interested in these little cars, and prices of the rare survivors slowly began to rise.

Before long another company started building a modern electric version (this had a reverse gear but there was still only one door and a single headlamp) and in America a collector paid **$176,000** for one of the originals. That's about **700** times what the little P50 cost when it was new, and not much less than you'd pay for a brand new Lamborghini.

FERRARI

250 GTO

FERRARI 250 GTO

THE FIFTY-MILLION-POUND FERRARI

» Only thirty-six were ever made

» A new one cost more than eight family cars

» . . . And second-hand the price is more than 8,000 times higher!

No one really knows which is the world's most valuable old car. It could be one of the Bugatti Royales (see page 32), the famous 1907 Rolls-Royce Silver Ghost or a race-winning Mercedes Grand Prix car from the 1930s. Parts of the Rolls-Royce were made of real silver and the ferociously fast Mercedes got their nickname – the Silver Arrows – because all the paint was stripped off their aluminium bodies in order to save a few hundred grams.

Fabulous cars like these are mostly displayed in museums nowadays. They rarely come up for sale so it's hard to know how much they're worth. But looking at prices of cars that have been sold, one name comes top of the list and it's not Bugatti, Rolls-Royce or Mercedes-Benz. In fact the name is Ferrari, and its prancing horse badge, can be found on nearly all of the most valuable classic cars ever sold.

Ferraris have always been fast but their early cars are also incredibly rare. These days the factory in Italy produces thousands of cars a year but in the beginning it made only a few dozen. Sometimes the company made more racing cars than road cars, and when these began to win the world's toughest, most famous races Ferrari grew to become one of the most glamorous brands in the world.

The Ferrari's fantastic handling and its hand-built 3.0 litre, 300 horsepower V12 helped the company win the World Sportscar Championships three years in a row.

In its seventy-year history its most valuable car is this one: the 250 GTO. It was manufactured between 1962 and 1964 and only thirty-six of them were ever made. Back then a top speed of **174 mph** made it the fastest car most people had ever seen. (The original Mini is almost the same age but like most cars then it struggled to hit **80 mph**.) The Ferrari's fantastic handling and its hand-built **3.0 litre, 300 horsepower** V12 helped the company to win the World Sportscar Championships three years in a row.

No-one knows why this particular car is so much more expensive than all the other Ferraris.

In 1962 a brand new GTO cost roughly **£6,000**, more than eight times the price of a family car like the Ford Consul Classic. Half a century later the most paid for a second-hand one is more than fifty million pounds, which is enough to buy around three thousand modern Fords. It's unlikely anyone would want that many, but there is one collector in England who has bought himself two of these stunning Ferraris.

The price will probably continue to climb even higher, but no one knows why this particular car is so much more expensive than all the others. It's certainly fast, rare and fabulous looking, but there are other Ferraris which are rarer than this one and quite a few which are faster. There might even be one or two Ferraris which are better looking, but the GTO is still the one most enthusiasts would buy if they could. The chance to own a genuine Ferrari racing car makes the GTO irresistible, and it must help that, unlike a Formula One car, it's possible to drive it around on normal roads.

Experts say the other part of its appeal is that although these cars are very rare they're not *too* rare. This means a lot of people know what a GTO looks like and they know how expensive it is to buy one. If it was any rarer owners might have to explain to their friends what they had bought, and why, which might be annoying for anyone who had just spent all that money.

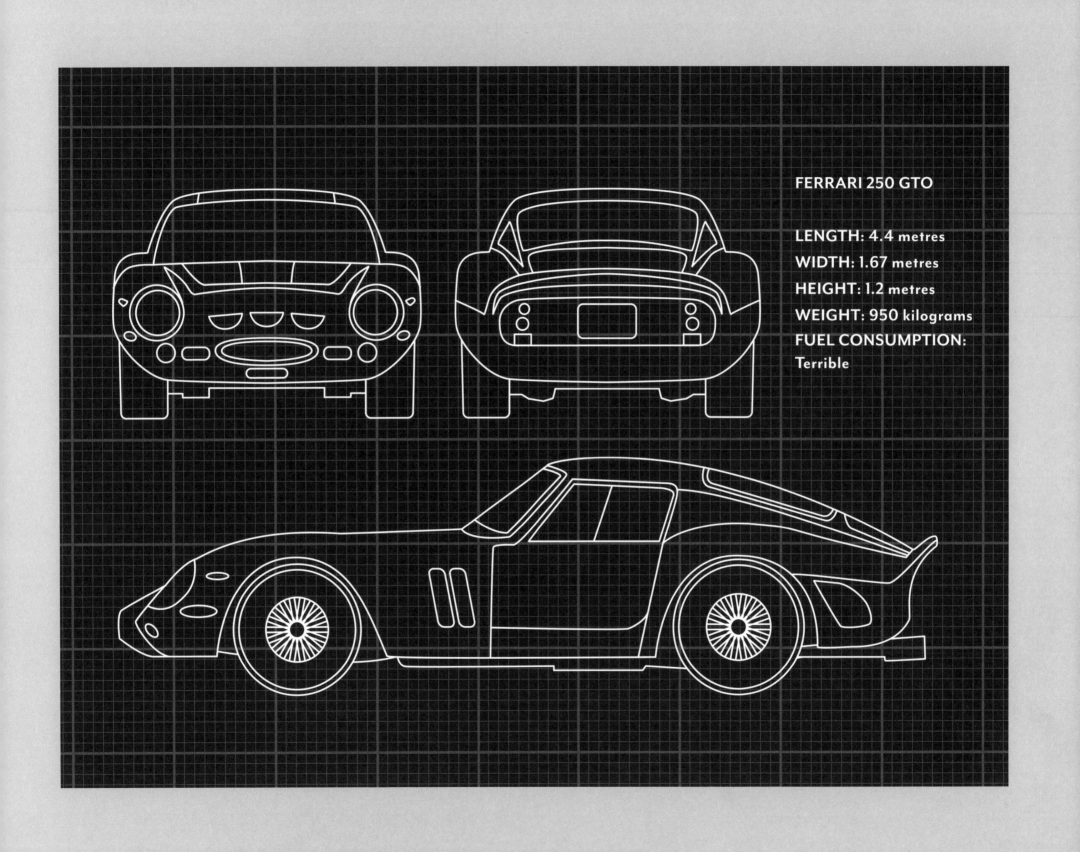

FERRARI 250 GTO

LENGTH: 4.4 metres

WIDTH: 1.67 metres

HEIGHT: 1.2 metres

WEIGHT: 950 kilograms

FUEL CONSUMPTION:
Terrible

LOCKHEED

S R - 71

LOCKHEED *SR-71*

THE FASTEST PLANE THAT EVER FLEW

» More than 2,000 mph – or thirty-six miles in under a minute

» On-board cameras could film 100,000 square miles in an hour

» . . . And spot a shoe from more than sixteen miles up.

Nicknamed the Blackbird, the incredible SR-71 spyplane stopped flying missions nearly twenty years ago but it's still the fastest jet ever built.

It was able to fly at more than three times the speed of sound so was much faster even than Concorde. The highest speed it ever recorded was a staggering **2,193.13 mph**, meaning it could fly thirty-six miles in less than a minute. In fact, aviation experts think it was probably even faster than this, but the true top speed is still a US government secret.

During missions Blackbirds frequently came under attack from America's enemies. None was ever shot down, however, largely because the Blackbirds were so fast that they could outrun any of the missiles that were fired at them.

It was vital it could do this because, as a spy plane, the SR-71 didn't have a single gun or bomb. To stay out of trouble pilots just had to fly higher and faster than any other aircraft. While they did this, special on-board cameras and

The Blackbirds were so fast that they could outrun any of the missles that were fired at them.

other top-secret equipment took pictures and collected information about military bases down below.

This equipment was so sensitive that even in broad daylight and parked on the runway the SR-71 could reportedly 'see' dozens of different stars. Flying at a height of sixteen miles, far higher than Concorde, the SR-71 could identify objects on the ground that were smaller than a shoe. Indeed, using just one of its cameras, the two-man crew could photograph **100,000 square miles** of the Earth's surface in a single hour, something which used up an incredible two miles of film per mission.

The plane's unusual shape made it almost impossible to spot on radar, and its special black paint helped cool down the temperature of the fuselage. This was necessary because flying at such high speeds aircraft become enormously hot. Blackbird's fuselage was made of titanium rather than aluminium but it still reached a temperature of nearly **500° Celsius**.

Because metal expands when it's heated the body panels were designed not to fit together perfectly at normal temperature. Bizarrely, this meant the plane constantly leaked fuel when it was parked on the runway. The only answer to this problem was for the SR-71 to take off with very little fuel in its tanks. It would then be refuelled in mid-air before going off on its top-secret mission.

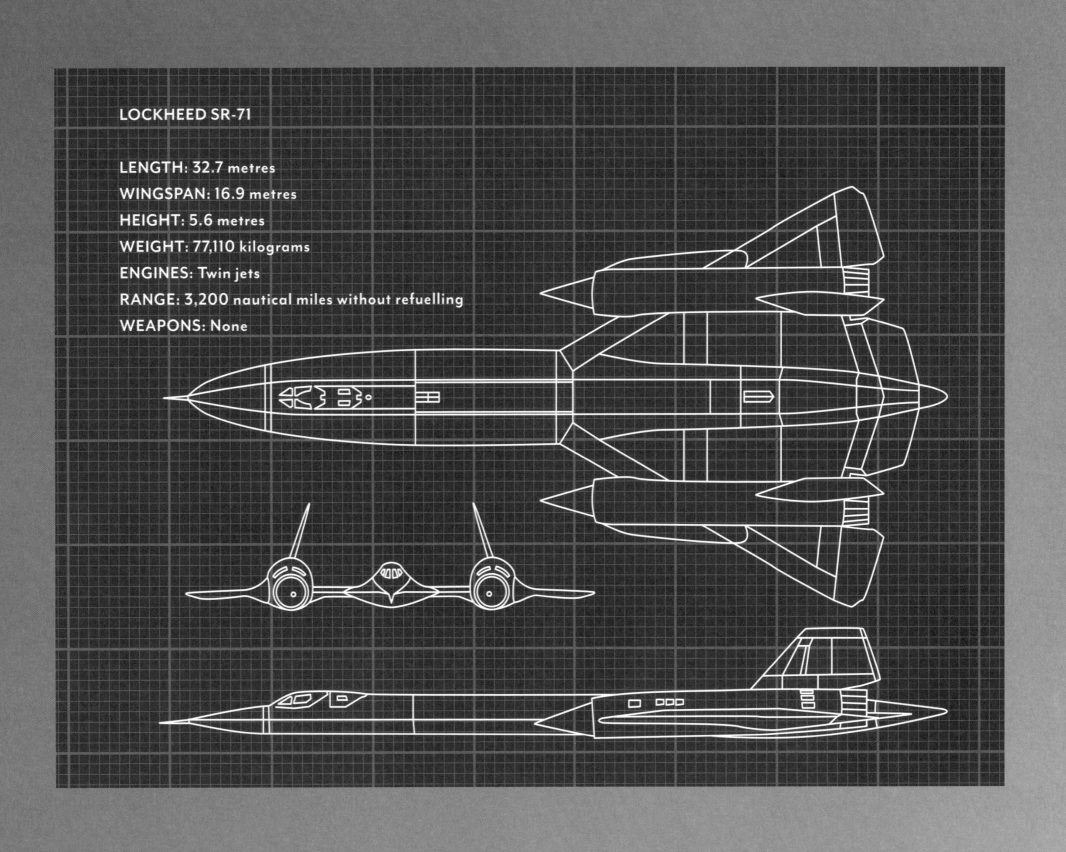

LOCKHEED SR-71

LENGTH: 32.7 metres
WINGSPAN: 16.9 metres
HEIGHT: 5.6 metres
WEIGHT: 77,110 kilograms
ENGINES: Twin jets
RANGE: 3,200 nautical miles without refuelling
WEAPONS: None

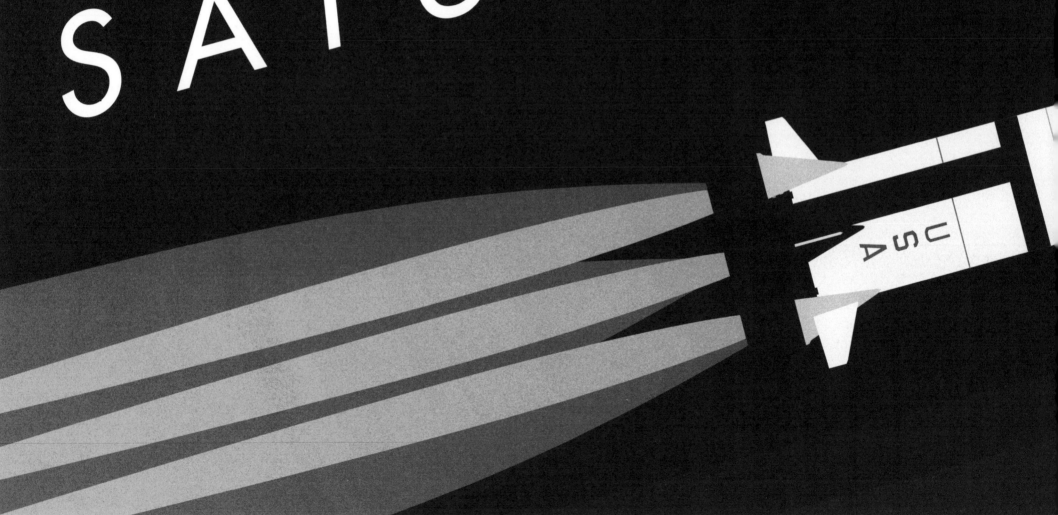

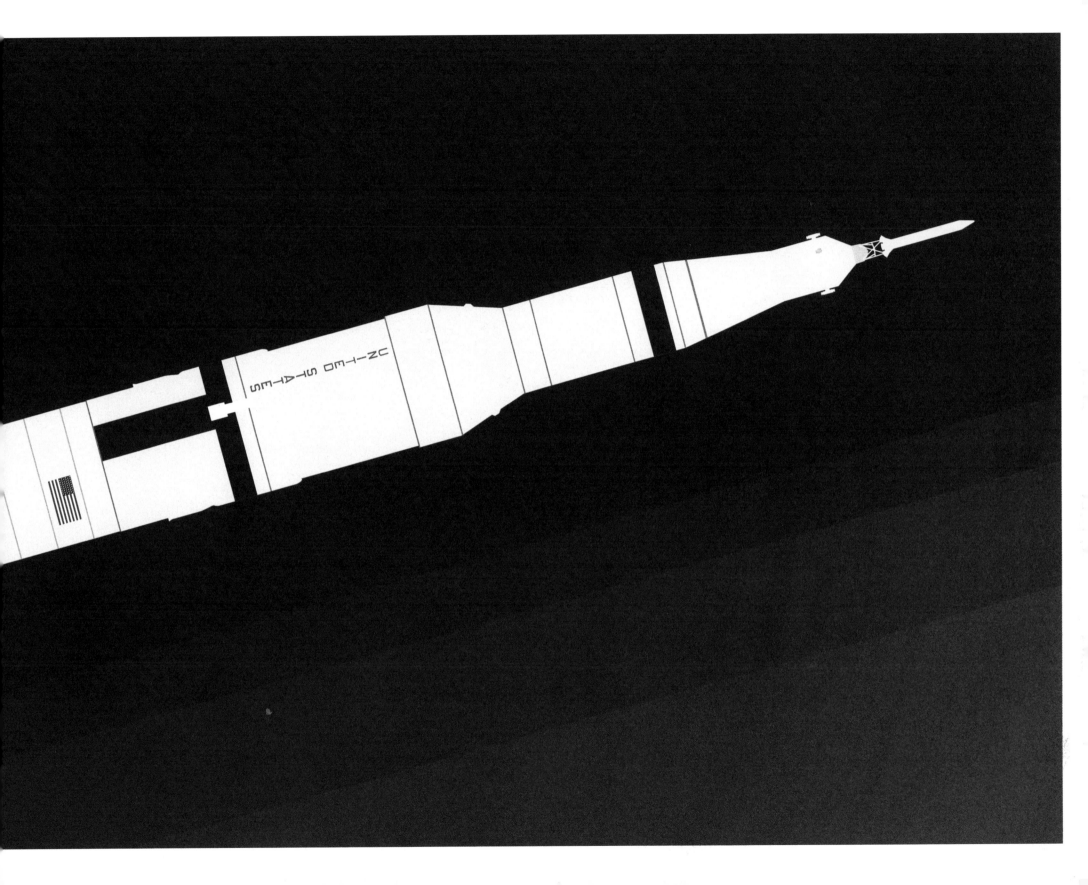

SATURN V

TO THE MOON AND BACK

» **The most expensive, most complex machine ever built**

» **110 metres from nose to tail**

» **. . . But barely enough room for a crew of three**

Hundreds of men and women have been into space, but only twenty-four people have flown all the way to the Moon and only half of them got to walk on its surface. America's Apollo astronauts flew there in Saturn V rockets, the tallest, heaviest and most powerful rockets that have ever flown.

More than fifty years after the first moonwalkers blasted into space, the Saturn V is still the most complicated and most expensive machine ever built. It cost the equivalent of **£170 billion** to put those twelve astronauts on the Moon – that's more than **£14 billion** each! The project to get them there safely (and back again) involved more than **400,000** scientists, engineers and mathematicians and each time a Saturn V was launched it cost hundreds of millions of pounds.

Each rocket was made of around three million parts and weighed 2,800 tonnes, which is about the same as a street of fifty houses.

Each rocket was made of around three million parts and weighed **2,800 tonnes**, which is about the same as a street of fifty houses. Stretching more than **110 metres** from nose to tail, a Saturn V on its launch pad stood much taller than either America's Statue of Liberty or the clock tower everyone calls Big Ben. But despite its huge size, there was room on board for only three astronauts at a time. Flying at more than **24,000 mph**, the three were squashed together for several days into a tiny capsule at the top which was not much larger than an ordinary car.

This capsule was the only part of the rocket designed to return to Earth. Most of the rest was taken up by eleven powerful rocket motors and several gigantic cylindrical tanks containing the fuel needed to fly a million miles. Rockets use a highly explosive combination of kerosene, hydrogen and oxygen instead of petrol or diesel, and they need lots of it to escape the Earth's gravitational pull. Once it was used up the part of the rocket containing the fuel was jettisoned and left behind to float around in space before eventually crashing down into the sea.

Following a launch all this happened incredibly quickly. A Saturn V burned ten times more fuel in its first *second* than Charles Lindbergh needed to become the first pilot to fly

Everything about flying to the Moon is dangerous, which is one of the reasons no-one has been back for nearly fifty years.

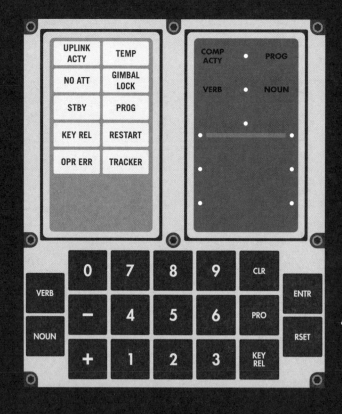

non-stop from America to Europe. In just a few minutes **3.5 million litres** of the mixture were used up. That's a million litres more than the water in an Olympic-sized swimming pool, or about the same amount of fuel a petrol station would need to fill the tanks of approximately **60,000** family cars.

With all this fuel and so many millions of tiny components, there was plenty to go wrong, and each time a Saturn V rocket was launched the spectators were kept three miles away in case it exploded. In fact, almost everything about flying to the Moon is dangerous, which is one of the reasons no one has been back for nearly fifty years. It's also why it took years of tests and practice flights before anyone was allowed to climb into a Saturn V and take off, and why it's still possible to see three of them today.

The first three Saturn rockets have survived because, instead of being launched, they were tested and retested to ensure that all the technology worked and was safe. This meant they never actually left the ground. The rest of them took off and were later abandoned out in space, but these precious examples of human inventiveness and ingenuity were carefully preserved and are now on display in museums in America.

BAC/AÉROSPATIALE
CONCORDE

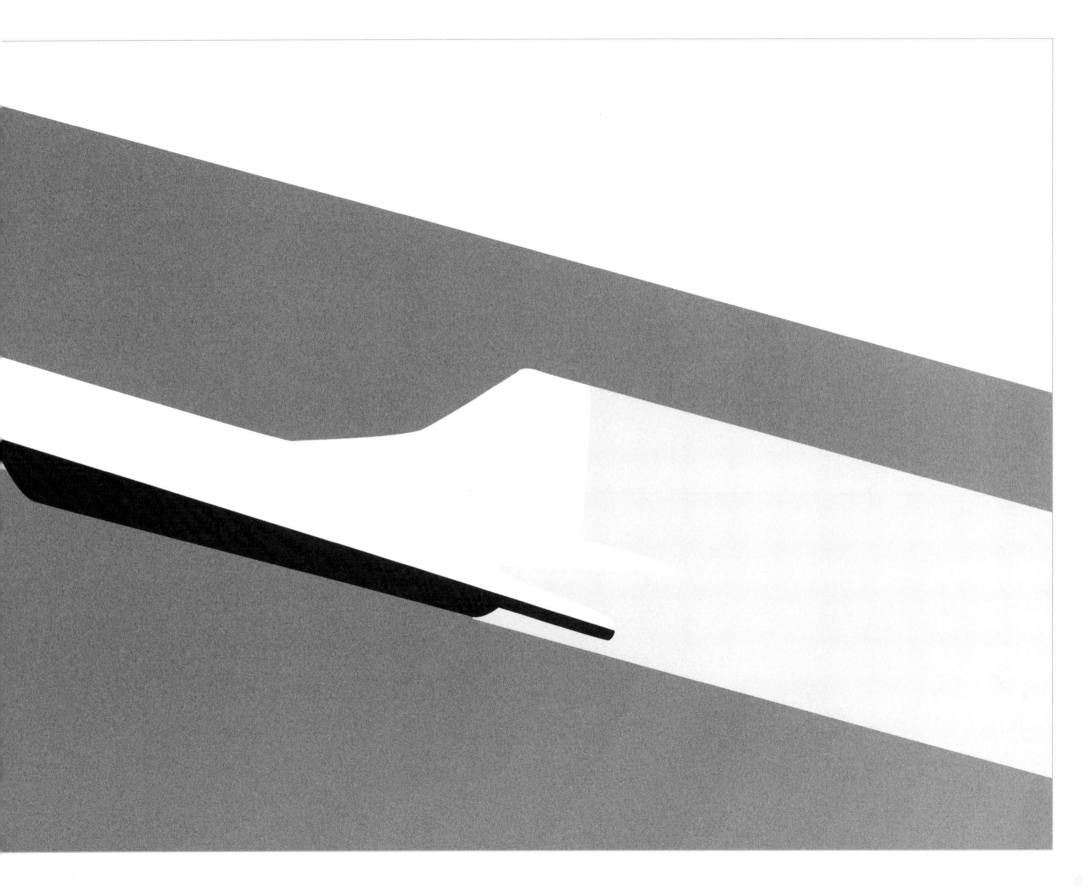

CONCORDE

FLYING FASTER THAN THE SPEED OF SOUND

» It flies so high it is close to the edge of space

» Flying so fast causes the body to heat up and expand in flight

» The noise is enough to shatter windows at ground level

Today the only way you can fly faster than the speed of sound is to become a pilot and join the air force. But for nearly thirty years anyone with enough money could buy a ticket for Concorde and fly from London to New York at more than **1,350 mph**.

Ordinary airliners cruise at around **500 mph** and they take about eight hours to cross from Europe to America. Concordes did it in under three, and in 1986 one of them managed to fly all the way round the world to set a new record. The first time anyone had attempted to do this in an aeroplane it took **175** days, but Concorde completed the journey in less than thirty hours.

Doing this meant flying at twice the speed of sound, and at a much higher altitude than any other airliner. Most of these fly about **10,000 metres** above sea level, which is approximately six miles high. Concorde could

When Concorde accelerated to the speed of sound (about 740 mph) it made a loud bang called a sonic boom.

fly as high as **18,000 metres**, which was so high that passengers could look down and see the curvature of the Earth. Looking up was even weirder. At this height the sky appeared almost black because Concorde was flying close to the edge of space!

Strange things happen when you fly this high and this fast. For a start Concorde burned more fuel in an hour (nearly **26,000 litres**) than the average family car uses in about two years. The body of the aircraft also got so hot when it did this that it expanded by thirty centimetres. It

shrank back to normal as it landed, but imagine being in a plane that gets larger and larger the faster it flies! Another strange thing was that the time difference between Britain and America meant passengers heading for New York seemed to arrive there before they had taken off . . .

Even with the extra thirty centimetres, however, Concorde was a lot smaller than most modern airliners and so it felt more cramped. The largest Airbus A380, for example, can accommodate up to **850** passengers on two levels, but Concorde had room for only **109** crew and passengers because its fuselage was much narrower. It was still quite luxurious though and when it first took to the air, passengers were served Champagne, caviar and lobster.

In 1979 Queen Elizabeth II flew to the Middle East on Concorde, making Her Majesty the world's first supersonic sovereign. Concorde was also popular with pop stars and celebrities, and in 1998 a **105**-year-old lady called Eva Woodman became its oldest ever passenger. There was also an American businessman who liked it so much that he used to make an average of three flights a week!

Fourteen Concordes carried 2.5 million passengers on 50,000 journeys.

Not everyone loved Concorde though. It was elegant and beautiful, but four powerful engines made it incredibly noisy and it produced terrible air pollution. When Concorde accelerated to the speed of sound (about **740 mph**) it made a loud bang called a sonic boom. This was so loud it could be heard more than sixty miles away, and the shock waves could actually shatter the windows of houses down on the ground.

Because of this, pilots were usually only allowed to fly fast when they were over the sea. For a while Concorde was forbidden to land in the USA, and the Saudi Arabians also complained, saying the noise upset their camels.

Altogether a fleet of fourteen Concordes carried **2.5 million** passengers on **50,000** journeys to more than **250** destinations. Unfortunately, after twenty-seven years without incident, one of the aircraft struck a small piece of metal lying on the runway at an airport outside Paris. A fire started on the aircraft and it crashed seconds later, killing everyone on board. It was the only accident involving one of these magnificent machines, but it was decided to retire Concorde. Today anyone wanting to board one has to visit a museum.

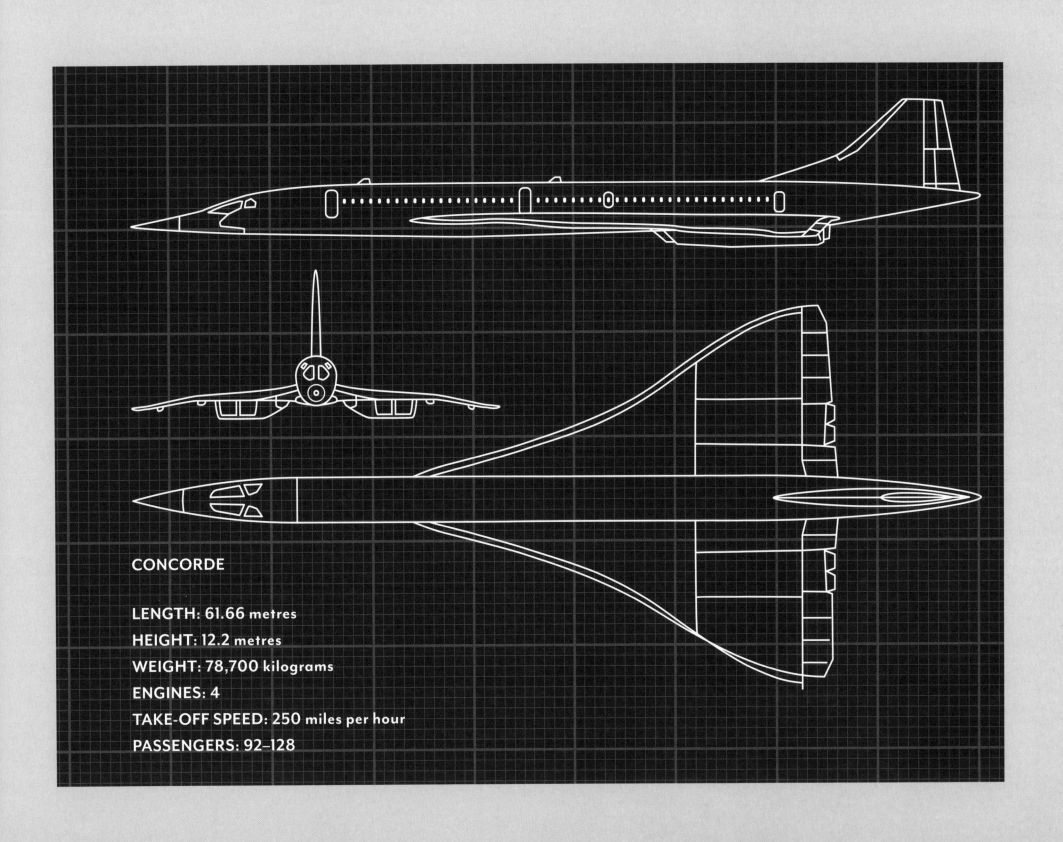

CONCORDE

LENGTH: 61.66 metres
HEIGHT: 12.2 metres
WEIGHT: 78,700 kilograms
ENGINES: 4
TAKE-OFF SPEED: 250 miles per hour
PASSENGERS: 92–128

LUNAR
ROVING
VEHICLE

LUNAR ROVER

THE CAR THAT DROVE ON THE MOON

» **The first car to go into outer space**

» **Each one cost millions of dollars to build**

» **Yet they were abandoned after driving just a few dozen miles**

The most expensive cars ever made cost millions of dollars each, yet three of them were left behind on the Moon.

Nicknamed Moon buggies, the four lunar rovers looked a bit like go-karts but were very different to ordinary cars. They had to be as light as possible, because launching anything into space costs a lot of money, and they had to fold down very small in order to fit into the spacecraft.

To help with this they had lightweight metal tyres instead of rubber ones, and were powered by batteries. A normal car engine needs air to work as well as fuel. Because there is no air on the Moon a normal engine wouldn't work. Instead, each wheel was fitted with its own small electric motor. Two more motors were used to steer the wheels which the driver controlled by moving a joystick located between the seats.

Their top speed was only 8 mph, and they weren't very comfortable, but the Moon's low gravity made driving around a lot of fun.

The buggies were designed as two-seaters because only two astronauts at a time visited the Moon. Their top speed was only about **8 mph**, and they weren't very comfortable, but the Moon's low gravity made driving around a lot of fun. If a wheel hit one of the small rocks littering the lunar surface, the buggy took off and flew through space for several metres before coming down to land with a soft bump.

The astronauts had to be very careful though. Their bulky spacesuits made it hard to do up the seatbelts, and even at very slow speeds there was a danger that a sharp turn would cause the buggy to flip over. Drivers also had to avoid getting lost, and photographs were used for direction-finding as there were no maps of the Moon at this time.

Although the astronauts were allowed to have some fun, the buggies were really designed to carry scientific equipment around and for collecting rock samples to bring back to Earth. During the course of the Apollo missions to the Moon three of the Rovers travelled a total of just over **38 miles**, at a cost of about **$1,000,000** a mile. The last one was never used and is now in a museum.

USS
NIMITZ

USS NIMITZ

A WARSHIP THE SIZE OF A TOWN

» More than 5,500 people live on board

» Has a deck large enough to park 1,200 cars

» Carries nearly 100 aircraft

The world's largest warship stretches a third of a kilometre from stem to stern and has more aircraft on board than half the world's national air forces. It's powered by two nuclear reactors that can run for an incredible twenty-four years without refuelling. This means the USS *Nimitz* could sail approximately **7.5 million miles** without stopping, or about three hundred times around the equator.

Like a small town, it is home to thousands of people. A total of **5,500** servicemen and women crew the ship or fly and maintain the aircraft. Everything they need has to be carried on board, including enough ingredients to cook **20,000** meals a day. The ship even has its own barber's shop, and every week an incredible **1,500** people queue up to have their hair cut.

Around ninety aircraft are stored and repaired in giant hangars beneath the deck – a deck so large that there's room to park more than **1,200** cars on it. In fact, it's so large that one aircraft can take off from it while another one is landing on the other end.

Before going out on missions the aircraft are brought up to deck level in one of four giant lifts. Once on deck the aircraft is fired off the ship using an enormous steam-powered catapult. This enables the pilot to take off using a much shorter runway than would be needed taking off

A total of 5,500 servicemen and women crew the ship or fly and maintain the aircraft.

in the normal way. When a plane returns, another gadget, called the hydraulic arresting gear, catches hold of a hook on the bottom of the aircraft so it can stop in the shortest possible distance. In this way the *Nimitz* can launch and land an incredible **240** aircraft in a single day – can you imagine the noise?

As well as fighter jets and bombers, the *Nimitz* carries different types of helicopter. These are equipped for medical evacuation and for search and rescue missions, and many have been used in humanitarian roles following natural disasters around the world. Other pilots patrol the sea around the ship. Their job is to defend *Nimitz* if it comes under attack from enemy aircraft, ships, boats or submarines.

Defence is an important part of every sailor's job because aircraft carriers are so huge that they present the enemy with an irresistible target. The *Nimitz* is as tall as a **23** storey building, and more than **75 metres** wide, so can be seen from many miles away. Its powerful nuclear reactors give it a higher cruising speed than an ordinary warship, but it still only does **35 mph**. Racing away from trouble is never an option so the crew has to be prepared for an attack long before one actually happens.

Many of the defence systems on the *Nimitz* are top secret but they are known to include sophisticated missiles which can be used against other ships, aircraft and submarines. It is also equipped for something called electronic warfare, which involves disrupting an enemy's radar and weapons systems, and destroying its ability to communicate effectively. Other technologies enable the captain to tell if any other ships or aircraft are in the same area, and to identify where they are long before they can actually be seen and before they can see the massive *Nimitz*.

Even when a warship is not taking part in a battle, life on board can be very dangerous. At least once, an aircraft has crashed on to the deck of the *Nimitz*, killing fourteen crew members and injuring dozens more. The explosion which followed the crash wrecked nineteen other aircraft. Another six were destroyed when one of the ship's big guns malfunctioned, causing a fire.

Building a replacement can take ten or twelve years, and the price is enormous.

Fortunately incidents like these are extremely rare. Apart from the tragic loss of life, no navy can afford to lose an aircraft carrier. Building a replacement can take ten or twelve years, and the price is enormous. The next generation of American aircraft carriers are expected to cost more than **£6 billion** each, and then as much as a billion more for the aircraft. This explains why there are so few aircraft carriers in the world (at the moment it is about three dozen) and why most countries can't afford to have even one of them.

TEREX

33-19 TITAN

TEREX 33-19 'TITAN'

A TRUCK THE SIZE OF A FACTORY

» World's largest, heaviest, most powerful truck

» Weighs 550 tonnes when fully loaded

» Taller than a block of flats

In Australia trucks known as 'road trains' can be up to thirty-five metres in length. The electric-car company Tesla built a truck that could do **0–60 miles an hour** in just over five seconds, and in India there's at least one of them which has seventy-two wheels. Even so, the king of the trucks is this one: Canada's Terex 33-19, known as the 'Titan'.

The truck was built in 1973 to work in an iron ore mine. It's retired now and has become a tourist attraction but, after more than forty years, it's still the largest, heaviest and most powerful truck in the world. It's also the only one of its kind ever made, perhaps because building another one would cost more than **£3 million**.

Iron ore is the name given to the rock that iron is extracted from before it can be used to make anything. Most of the iron is needed to produce steel, which is used to manufacture everything from knives and forks to motor cars and skyscrapers. Because so many industries around the world use so much steel (more than one and a half billion tonnes every year) huge amounts of the rock have to be pulled out of the earth and processed.

It is the only one of its kind ever made, perhaps because building another one would cost more than £3 million.

The processing involves crushing the rock and heating up until the iron inside it melts and flows out. This is done in giant furnaces called smelters, which 'cook' the ore at very high temperatures to drive out its impurities. Because such a lot of iron ore is needed to make pure iron, and an awful lot of iron is needed to make steel, these mines are enormous places.

The largest one in the world is at Kiruna in northern Scandinavia. It covers many square miles and so far nearly a billion tonnes of rock have been dug out of the ground and processed. Unfortunately this has left such a large hole that the local town was in danger of falling into it. Tens of thousands of people living there have had to be moved to a new town two miles away.

Naturally really huge machines are needed to dig out half a million tonnes of rock every week, and special trucks are used to haul the iron ore away. The Titan, the largest of them all, is about the size of a four-storey block of flats: over twenty metres long, and seventeen metres tall with its dumper raised. It weighs more than many buildings though, and fully loaded it used to tip the scales at just under **550 tonnes**. Even the wheels and tyres are gigantic – nearly four metres in diameter – and all ten of them could be used to steer.

The driver's cab is located on the second storey, about six metres off the ground. It can only be reached by climbing a ladder which is larger than the staircase in a normal house. The Titan was surprisingly fast, though, and could be driven at nearly **30 mph**, although it was far too large to be driven on a proper road.

The secret to its impressive performance was a mighty turbocharged diesel engine.

The secret to its impressive performance was a mighty turbocharged diesel engine, a **169-litre**, sixteen-cylinder type usually used for pulling railway trains. Nearly twenty-five times larger than Ferrari's biggest ever engine, this produced more than **3,300 horsepower** but unusually the Titan didn't use it to turn the wheels. Instead the engine powered a generator that supplied electricity to several massive motors which turned the eight rear wheels. This is similar to the way a modern hybrid car works, although no one ever pretended the Titan was very green!

TEREX 33-19

WEIGHT: 550 tonnes fully loaded

HEIGHT: 17 metres

ENGINE: 169 litres diesel-electric

MAXIMUM POWER: 3,300 horsepower

NUMBER BUILT: One

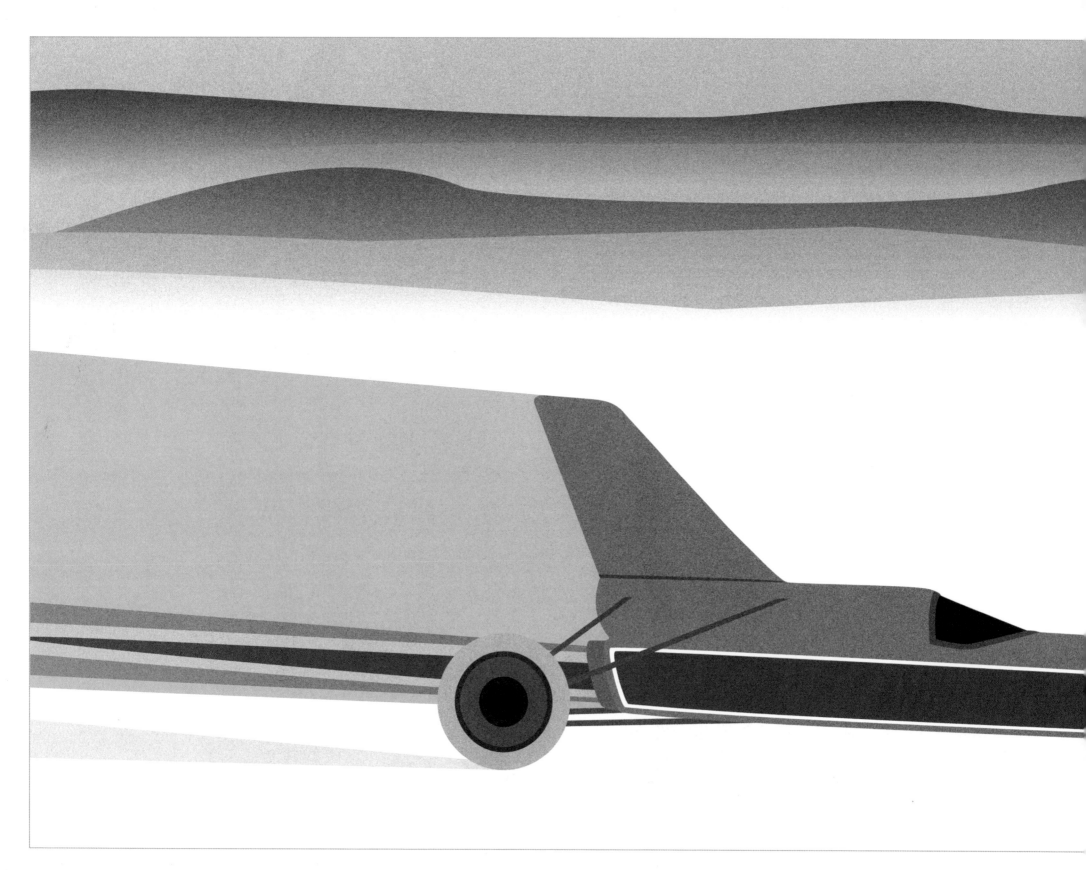

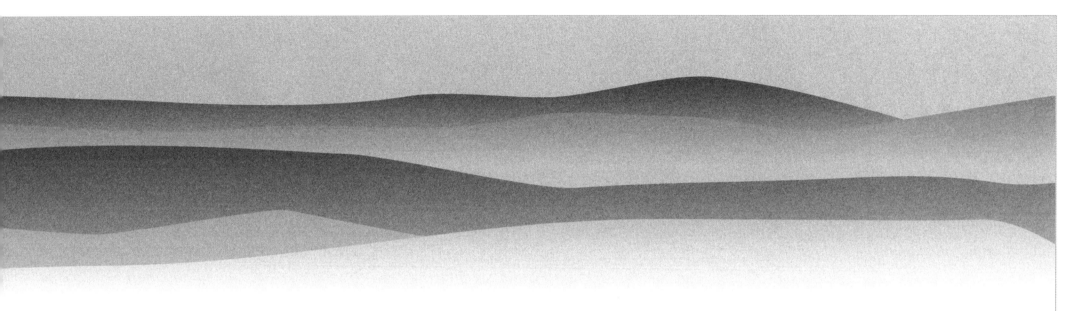

SMI

MOTIVATOR

SM1 MOTIVATOR

THE FASTEST WOMAN ON EARTH

» **512 mph across a dried-out lake bed**

» **Two massive engines – one from a rocket**

» **Less than half a second to cover 100 metres**

More than forty years ago Kitty Hambleton became the fastest woman on the planet after piloting her rocket-powered car at **512.710 mph** across a wide, empty stretch of America's Alvord Desert.

Kitty is a remarkable woman. Part Irish and part Native American, she became deaf as a child but went on to work in Hollywood as a stuntwoman. She was also a champion swimmer and had hoped to represent the United States in the Olympics until doctors treating her for cancer and spinal problems advised her to slow down. Slowing down wasn't really Kitty's style, however, and having developed a taste for excitement and adventure, she set her mind to breaking records of a different kind. Kitty tried racing various cars, bikes and even high-speed boats, and before long found herself talking to the builder of a really wild machine called the SM1 Motivator. This twelve-metre-long three-wheeler had two massive engines squeezed into its slender, needle-like body. The first engine produced **48,000 horsepower**, which is more than twice as much power as all the cars in a Formula One race put together. The second wasn't quite as big but it wasn't exactly weedy either. In fact it was a genuine rocket motor from a **2,000 mph** 'Sidewinder' missile.

Kitty and the car's owner planned an attempt on the women's world land speed record.

Together Kitty and the car's owner planned an attempt on the women's world land speed record, which they believed could be pushed to more than **500 mph**.

As you can imagine, cars like the Motivator are much too fast to be used on an ordinary race track. Instead the team headed for the beautiful state of Oregon. Although this lies on the coast of the Pacific ocean, it has some of the most arid places anywhere in the world. One of these, the Alvord Desert, is a dried-out lake bed, a wide, flat and desolate area which used to be an emergency landing strip for the US air force.

America has lots of these dry lake beds and a long history of using them for high-speed record tests. The one at Alvord looked perfect for Kitty and the amazing Motivator. The ground is hard and flat for miles around, much of it made of compacted salt left behind when the water in the lake evaporates. Almost nothing can grow in such a harsh environment so drivers don't have to worry about hitting a plant or a root poking above the smooth surface. That's important because when a vehicle is travelling at a very high speed hitting even the smallest object could spell disaster.

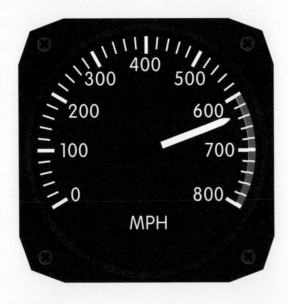

and she reached a speed of **300 mph**. (That's about twice as fast as a jet airliner is going when it takes off.) The following day she did it again, several times, gradually nudging her speed up towards **400 mph**!

Each run took only a few seconds to complete because a car travelling at **400 mph** takes only half a second to cover nearly **100 metres**. But between each attempt the team spent several hours preparing the car and doing everything they could to ensure Kitty's safety.

Kitty's record attempt took place in 1976, and on the morning of 3 December she was strapped into the cockpit for the first of several practice runs. The test went perfectly

In official record attempts like this only one vehicle is involved at a time. Even if there were two cars in the world capable of going fast enough, the risk of one hitting the other would make a race far too dangerous. Instead

Kitty raced 'against the clock'. This involves driving over a measured distance of one mile while timing equipment located at either end accurately records the time taken to as little as a thousandth of a second. Each run has to be repeated in the opposite direction and by taking an average of both runs it is possible to calculate a vehicle's true speed while ruling out any effects of wind or sloping ground.

At one point the car was actually travelling at more than 600 mph.

Eventually, on the fourth day, Kitty made her final attempt. This time her two-way average was the best yet: **512.710 mph** – easily a new world record. At one point the car was actually travelling at more than **600 mph**, but unfortunately for official record attempts only the average speed counts.

Altogether the amazing Kitty Hambleton went on to break twenty-two different records, on both land and water. This one, by far her most impressive, is still unbroken after more than four decades.

MACCREADY

GOSSAMER ALBATROSS

WITHDRAWN

GOSSAMER ALBATROSS

THE SLOWEST PLANE

» **Weighed half as much as its pilot**

» **Powered by pedals**

» **Made mostly of plastic**

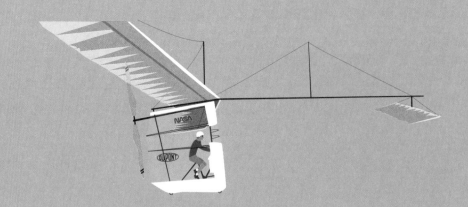

Almost certainly the slowest aeroplane ever built, the Gossamer Albatross was powered by a man on a bicycle instead of an engine. Bryan Allen used it in 1979 to become the first person to fly across the English Channel in a human-powered aircraft.

Bryan planned to do it by using his leg muscles to turn a large two-bladed propeller. This meant his aircraft had to be as light as possible, so American aeronautical engineer Paul MacCready designed one weighing just **32 kilograms**. That's the same as an average ten-year-old child, or about half what its pilot weighed at the time.

To achieve this Paul built a slender carbon fibre skeleton which he covered in thin, transparent plastic sheeting. The wings were made of ordinary expanded polystyrene, and they were exceptionally long like the wings of a glider. Each one was nearly fifteen metres from end to end, giving the

Albatross a wingspan almost the same as three London buses parked end to end.

Its maximum speed was expected to be **18 mph** but this required perfect weather. It also required Bryan to keep pedalling at quite a fast rate – at least **75 revolutions a minute** – and to keep it up all the way across the Channel.

On a day with little wind and a calm, flat sea, Bryan set off at six o'clock in the morning. With a support crew following in a boat below, he was soon flying about two metres above sea level. Almost immediately his radio failed, meaning that the only way he could communicate with the crew was by using hand signals. He also ran out of drinking water and soon began to feel dehydrated. This led to cramps in his legs which made it difficult and painful to pedal as fast as he needed to.

He had covered 22.2 miles at just under 8 mph.

After a couple of hours he was becoming exhausted, and the crew in the boat considered towing him the rest of the way. Bryan was determined to press on, however, and decided to fly slightly higher in the hope that there would be less turbulence up there. This worked brilliantly: before long he could see France and was soon able to float down to land on a sandy beach. His total flight time was **2 hours and 49 minutes**, meaning he had covered **22.2 miles** at just under **8 mph**. This was far slower than everyone had hoped for, but Gossamer Albatross had conquered the Channel.

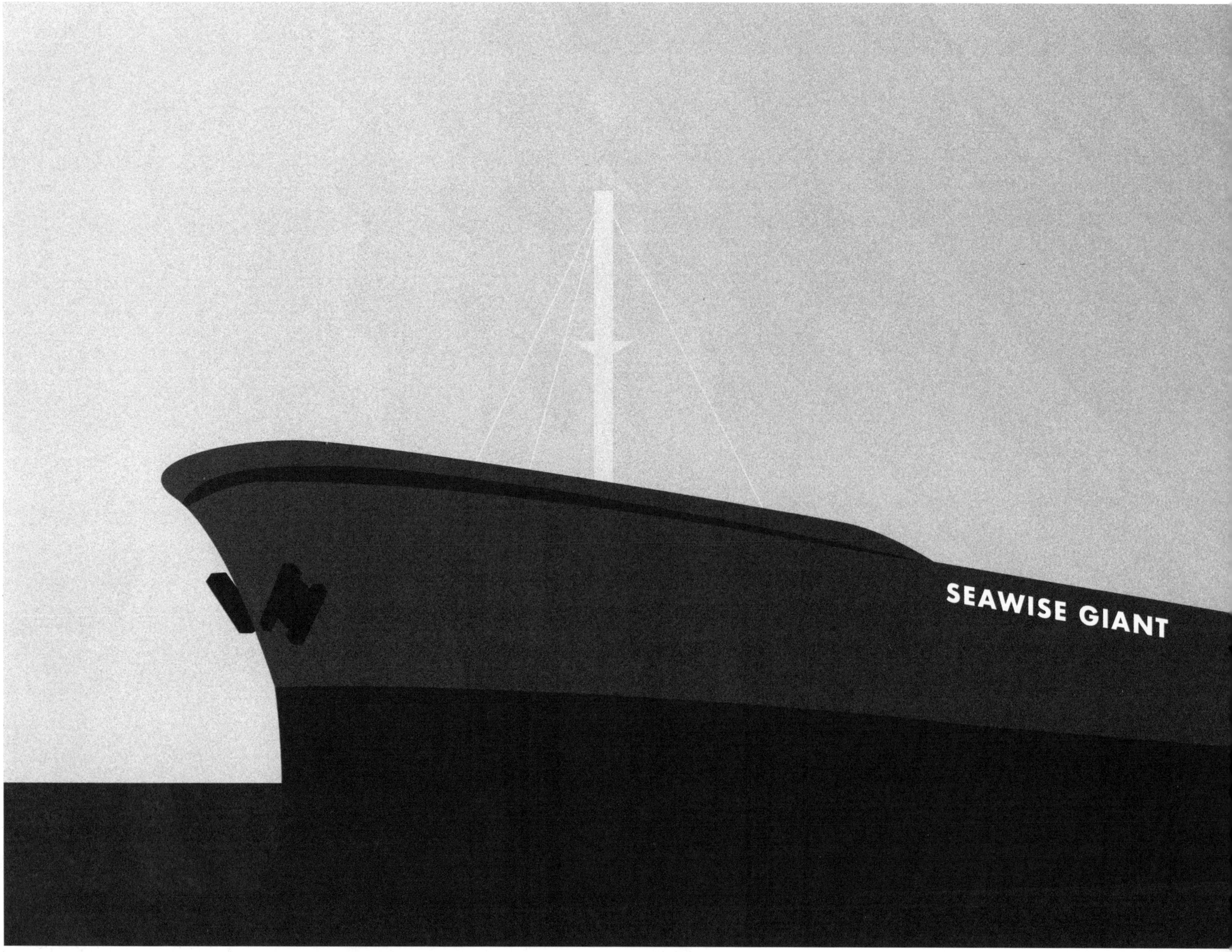
SEAWISE GIANT

SUMITOMO HEAVY INDUSTRIES
SEAWISE GIANT

SEAWISE GIANT

HALF A MILLION TONNES – BUT IT FLOATS!

» **The largest moving object ever made**

» **Too big to fit in any harbour**

» **Weighed more than the population of New York**

Seawise Giant, the largest ship ever built, was nearly half a kilometre long, and weighed an astonishing **564,763 tonnes** when fully loaded. That's about the same as nine million average-sized adults, so the ship weighed about the same as the entire population of London, Paris or New York.

The ship was a very special type of oil tanker called an 'ultra large crude carrier' (or ULCC). It's so big it took five years to build. When it was launched in 1979 the main deck was so long that there was room on there to lay down the Sears Tower, the world's tallest building at that time. Until it was scrapped thirty years later the ship was the largest moving man-made object in history, and even now there is still nothing out there to beat it.

Just over **458 metres** from end to end, and wider than six tennis courts, *Seawise Giant* had room in its forty-six tanks

to carry around **300 million litres** of oil, the equivalent of more than half a billion pints of beer. The oil was transported to dozens of countries around the world, although the ship was far too large to enter any port. Instead the oil had to be transferred to other, smaller tankers each time it was ready to unload.

As you can imagine, ships this large are extremely awkward to manoeuvre, and even with its **230-tonne** rudder *Seawise Giant* needed more than two miles of open ocean to turn round in. Slowing it down was also difficult and took a lot of time. When the captain wanted to stop the ship he had to switch off the two **50,000 horsepower** engines when he was still miles out at sea. These powered a fifty-tonne propeller that was nine metres in diameter, but even without this turning it took another twenty minutes for the ship to actually stop moving. In that time it would have drifted another five miles . . .

Unsurprisingly *Seawise Giant* was also massively expensive to build and operate. In fact it was so expensive that when it was bombed and sunk during the Iran–Iraq War a company in Norway decided to save it. Somehow they managed to refloat the wreck, which was then towed nearly **4,000 miles** from the Persian Gulf to Singapore. Over the next two years it was painstakingly rebuilt before being sold to a new owner.

The ship carried on working but by 2010 it was too old and inefficient to be used anymore. *Seawise Giant* made its final voyage to India where there are companies which specialise in scrapping huge ships of this sort. The whole ship was sadly broken up. The **36-tonne** main anchor was saved and taken to a museum in Singapore. Other parts and materials were recycled, a task which took more than **500** workers nine months to complete.

SEAWISE GIANT

BEDE AVIATION

BD - 5 J

BD-5J

BUILDING A JET FROM A KIT

» **The world's smallest jet aircraft**

» **Starred in a James Bond film**

» **Faster than a Formula One car**

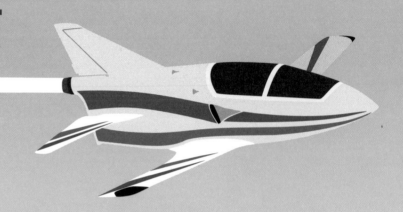

The world's smallest jet aircraft was the BD-5J. It was designed to be built from a kit at home, and one of them had a starring role in a James Bond film.

In the opening scene of *Octopussy*, the secret agent has an amazing, bullet-shaped aircraft hidden in a horsebox which he is towing behind a car. It looks like a toy but is incredibly fast, and after taking off Bond manages to dodge a deadly missile and avoid being captured by his enemies.

In the most spectacular scene of the film he flies just a few metres above ground level before aiming the BD-5J into a nearby aircraft hangar. When 007 is flying around inside the building the bad guys attempt to trap him by sliding the hangar doors closed at the other end. But Bond manages to escape by slipping through the narrowest of gaps after flipping the plane through ninety degrees and flying out sideways.

A top speed of around 300 mph meant the BD-5J was still a lot faster than a Formula One car.

It's a really brilliant stunt and was done without computers or any trick photography. But then the BD-5J is a brilliant little aeroplane. Jim Bede, its American inventor, became famous after designing an ultra-small propeller plane which enthusiasts could build themselves in their garden sheds. It was only just large enough for the pilot (no bags or passengers) but it was astonishingly cheap. The whole kit cost less than the price of a small car.

Amateur pilots loved the idea of building their own flying machines and thousands of them bought kits and plans from Jim's company. When he said he was thinking of making a much more powerful jet version, a lot of them liked this idea too. Keen to press on, he began to modify the original design to make it faster and even sleeker.

Jim knew this project was going to be a difficult one, and not just because most jet engines at the time were quite a lot larger than his entire aeroplane. Eventually he found a company in France which made a really small one. This could be fitted into his prototype without ruining its sleek appearance. Most home-made aeroplanes are a bit boxy or awkward-looking, but the styling of the BD-5J was more like that of a proper, miniature fighter jet. It looked fantastic whether it was flying around or just sitting on the runway.

The pilot had to lie down to fit beneath the clear, plastic canopy, and the jet engine was located immediately behind his head. It made a lot of noise but didn't produce much power, although in such a light and aerodynamic machine this didn't really matter. A top speed of around **300 mph** meant the BD-5J was still a lot faster than a Formula One car and much, much faster than the old propeller version had been.

Jim's new creation attracted a lot of attention even before anyone had seen the Bond film. People were desperate to buy the kits, and one man bought twenty of them to start a business building aircraft for pilots who didn't have the time, space or skills to build their own at home.

Before long several BD-5Js were performing exciting flying displays at air shows across America and Canada. They included a couple which flew in formation as the *Silver Bullets*, and the actual aeroplane from *Octopussy* quickly

Jim's tiny little machines are still flying more than forty years later.

became one of the star attractions. Unfortunately it later crashed when the engine caught fire, but luckily the pilot was able to bail out before using his parachute to drift safely down to the ground.

No one knows how many of the kits were actually finished and flown because building your own jet at home turned out to be harder than it sounds. But several of Jim's tiny little machines are still flying more than forty years later. Their small size means they are extremely hard to spot on a radar screen so at least one of them has been used to train American military personnel to shoot down cruise missiles.

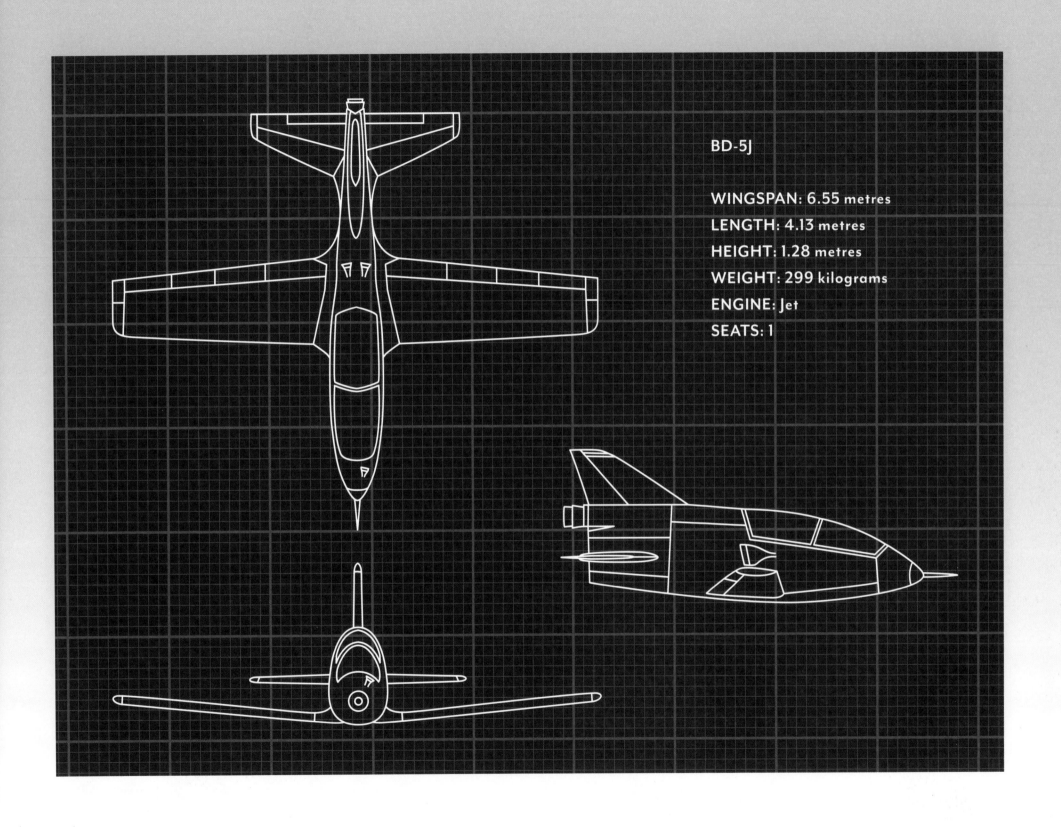

BD-5J

WINGSPAN: 6.55 metres

LENGTH: 4.13 metres

HEIGHT: 1.28 metres

WEIGHT: 299 kilograms

ENGINE: Jet

SEATS: 1

BELL BOEING

V-22 OSPREY

BELL BOEING OSPREY

HISTORY'S MOST EXPENSIVE HELICOPTER

» **The most expensive helicopter in the world**

» **Drops spies behind enemy lines**

» **Can travel a thousand miles without refuelling**

The most expensive helicopter in the world doesn't really look much like a helicopter at all. The Bell Boeing V-22 Osprey takes off vertically and it has giant rotor blades, but there's something about its appearance when it swoops low over the ground which makes it look a lot more like an ordinary aeroplane.

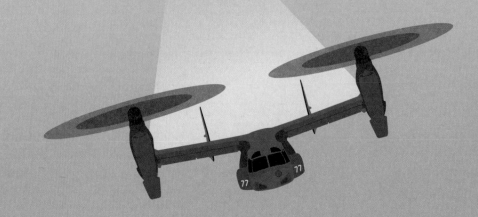

There is, however, nothing ordinary about the Osprey, which was designed to combine the speed of an aeroplane with the abilities of a helicopter. Being able to take off and land without a runway makes military helicopters perfect for jungle, mountain and desert warfare, and for rescuing injured troops trapped behind enemy lines. But they are usually a lot slower than most aeroplanes, which puts the crew at greater risk of being shot down. Another drawback is that most of them can't fly very far before running out of fuel.

With a top speed of over 350 mph, the Osprey is at least 150 mph faster than a normal helicopter.

The astonishing Osprey avoids these problems by using an ingenious gadget called a 'tiltrotor'. When the rotors are pointing upwards the horizontal blades make it possible to take off and land like a helicopter, and to do this almost anywhere. Then, once it is airborne, the rotors tilt forward, putting the blades into a vertical position so that they work like gigantic propellers. In this position they give the Osprey a top speed of more than **350 mph**, which is at least **150 mph** faster than a normal helicopter.

Its two gigantic Rolls-Royce engines develop **12,300 horsepower** and the Osprey can fly more than a thousand miles without having to refuel. Additional fuel tanks are sometimes fitted to give it an even greater range for secret missions, and where necessary it can even be refuelled in mid-air. If one engine fails it can still fly using the other one, and amazingly, in the unlikely event that both break down, it can glide safely back down to earth.

Designing something this new and innovative usually costs more than people think, and so the American government set aside a whopping **$2.5 billion (£2 billion)** to fund the Osprey project. In the end even this was nowhere near enough money. The final bill was nearly twenty-five times larger than expected, meaning that each new machine costs around twice the price of the military helicopter it was designed to replace.

A high top speed means it can fly behind enemy lines without being detected.

Even at this massive price though it is a hugely impressive machine. It's so complex that it takes a crew of four to fly it (most helicopters need only one or two), and so big that there's room on board for thirty-two fully armed marines or nine tonnes of military supplies. Even with all of that there's enough space left for a rugged off-road vehicle, which soldiers call the Growler.

When you first see it, the little Growler looks similar to a Jeep. And like a Jeep, it can be used as an attack vehicle or to tow weapons into battle. But unlike a Jeep, sophisticated electronics fitted to one version mean it can be operated by remote control, something which makes the Growler ideal for use in situations where a manned vehicle would be too dangerous. Other Growlers can be programmed to follow soldiers wearing beacons or tracking devices which send out special electronic signals.

With or without the Growler, though, the real key to the Osprey's success is its versatility. It can perform multiple different roles in many different situations. A high top speed means it can fly behind enemy lines without being detected. By using something called terrain-following radar it can also fly exceptionally low, just a few metres above the ground, while automatically avoiding obstacles such as trees and hills.

Together with sophisticated night-vision equipment this makes the Osprey perfect for Special Forces work, such as dropping secret agents deep into hostile territory. Ospreys are also used for search-and-rescue operations, for example when recovering pilots who have crashed on the battlefield. Amazingly sophisticated electronics mean it can hover automatically while a crew member is winched down to bring the airman back on board. Other Ospreys work as submarine hunter-destroyers, as air-ambulances to ferry injured troops (or civilians caught up in natural disasters) to safety, and for airborne early-warning to detect enemy aircraft more than **200 miles** away.

The Osprey is frequently transported by ship, as an important part of the modern US Marines Corps armoury. It is one of the largest machines which can travel this way, and can only do so because of its clever wing design. This enables the wings to swivel round, and with its rotors folded the **17-metre-long** machine can then be stored not just on the largest US navy aircraft carriers but also on much smaller warships as they steam into action.

BAGGER

293

BAGGER 293

THE WORLD'S LARGEST LAND VEHICLE

» **Twice as long as a football pitch**

» **Can dig out twelve tonnes of rock every second**

» **. . . But it would take all day to drive less than a mile**

The largest land vehicle ever made is the Bagger 293, a type of monster digger known as a bucket-wheel excavator.

It took five years just to build this German giant and it cost more than **£75 million**. When it was finished, the Bagger weighed **14,200 tonnes** – which is about the same as ninety jumbo jets. With a height of **96 metres** it's the world's tallest land vehicle. It's also the longest at **225 metres**, and (perhaps unsurprisingly) one of the slowest. A few years ago the Bagger took more than three weeks to travel less than fourteen miles.

Although the Bagger is more than twice as long as a football pitch it needs only five people to operate it. They use it to dig out material from a coal mine, which it does faster and more efficiently than anything else. Excavating twelve tonnes a second, in a single day it can remove

240 **million litres** of soil, stone and coal. That's enough to fill 96 Olympic swimming pools or an incredible **2,500** railway wagons forming a train nearly twenty miles long.

At one end of the machine is a giant wheel more than **21 metres** in diameter. This is fitted with eighteen vast scoops or buckets. As the wheel turns these take great, six-tonne bites out of the Earth, dumping the coal on to a long conveyor belt which runs to the back of the machine. From there several more miles of conveyors move the coal away from the mine and on to trains which take it to three nearby power stations. These generate electricity, much of which is then fed back to power the Bagger 293 as it digs out more coal.

The machine itself is highly efficient and does all the digging, but anyone working on it has to be extremely fit as

The Bagger has more than 2000 steps and half a mile of walkways.

well. With numerous ladders and stairways, the Bagger has more than **2,000** steps and half a mile of walkways. Every day each member of the crew walks about six miles, although someone has calculated that without the machine it would take **40,000** men to dig out the same amount of coal using only spades.

HEXIE HAO

TRAINS THAT LOOK AND GO LIKE ROCKETS

» **Nearly 250 mph, and that's with the brakes on!**

» **14,000 miles of track**

» **1.5 billion passengers a year**

The subway trains running under London, Paris and New York rarely move at more than **20 mph**, but in other parts of the world trains are travelling faster and faster.

The highest speed recorded by one of these is an amazing **374 mph**, in Japan in 2015, but the fastest regular service is now operated by the Chinese. China is a vast country of nearly **1.4 billion** people and has more of these high-speed, long-distance trains than any other country. It also has the world's largest and most expensive high-speed rail network. Travelling along more than **14,000 miles** of high-speed track, its trains travel at around **220 mph** with occasional bursts of up to **248 mph**. (They can do **300 mph** but regulations don't allow it.)

At this sort of a speed it would take one of these trains less than an hour to travel from London to Paris, and just over nine hours to cross the whole of the United States from one side to the other. Aeroplanes are faster but trains can carry far more people and, in a single year, China sells around one and a half billion tickets to people wanting to use its high-speed service. Trains are also a very safe way to travel, although in 2011 one in China was struck by lightning.

The country's longest high-speed line runs from the capital Beijing to the city of Shenzhen on the coast. That's an incredible **1,372 miles**, which is further than the distance from London to the Arctic Circle. Eventually the line will reach all the way to Hong Kong, by which time it will have taken more than seven years to build.

To travel this fast the trains have to be sleek and streamlined. From the front their long noses make them look a bit like jet airliners, and the experience of riding in one of them is very much like being on board an aircraft.

Every year China sells around one and a half billion tickets for its high-speed service.

The view through their much larger windows can be spectacular, especially when another train comes the other way. If both trains are travelling at maximum speed they flash by each other at a combined speed equivalent to more than **450 miles an hour**.

Although travelling this way is cheap and luxurious, passengers do have one complaint. Apparently the trains go so quickly that it is hard to make a telephone call without losing the signal.

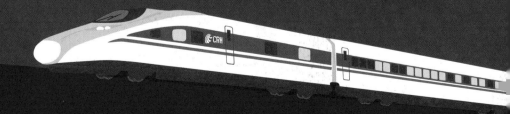

BLOODHOUND LSR

BLOODHOUND LSR

1,000 MPH ACROSS THE DESERT

» **Travels a mile in only 3.6 seconds . . .**

» **. . . and takes more than five miles to slow down**

» **It's faster than a bullet fired from a gun**

The Bloodhound LSR is the best attempt yet to build a **1,000 mph** car. It's the brainchild of two Englishmen who have outstanding track records when it comes to driving insanely fast.

One of them, engineer Richard Noble, captured the world land speed record nearly forty years ago by driving at an astonishing **633.47 mph** across America's Nevada desert. A few years later he came back with an even faster car, this time driven by Royal Air Force pilot Andy Green. Green's plan was not merely to beat Richard's record but to break the sound barrier – which he did by posting an average speed of **763.035 mph**.

You might think because many military jets are faster than this, all anyone would have to do to break the record is to take the wings off one and call it a car. In fact this has been tried, but so far the best speed anyone has managed is just under **400 mph**. Clearly it takes a bit more than a wingless fighter jet to break the record, even when it boasts **52,000** horsepower.

Richard and Andy set out to build a third, entirely new machine instead, which they called the Bloodhound LSR. This also uses the jet engine from a plane, but a much, much more powerful one. It's of a newer type too, borrowed from the latest RAF Eurofighter, and is joined by three rocket motors, each of which produces more power than all twenty of the cars taking part in this year's Formula One World Championship. In total the driver has **135,000 horsepower** to play with, which is more than the *QE2*, one of the largest and most luxurious ocean liners ever built, had.

So try and imagine a car so powerful that if it was launched into the air like a firework it would reach a height of nearly five miles before falling back to earth. That's higher than nearly all of the world's tallest mountains, and with all that power it should be possible to get from zero to a thousand miles an hour in less than a minute.

To do it, to break the record, Andy will need to travel a mile in just **3.6 seconds**, or the length of four football pitches in less than one. At that sort of speed the four gigantic titanium wheels attached to the **12.9 metre-long** vehicle will need to spin round more than **10,000** times a minute. To do that requires an immense amount of power as well as an incredibly advanced form of fuel, called high-test peroxide (HTP).

Richard and Andy believe HTP is greener than conventional fuels because when it breaks down it produces only steam and oxygen. But it's also highly dangerous and so corrosive that every single component which comes into contact with it has to be made of a special material which has been 'pickled' in an acid bath to remove any potentially dangerous contaminants.

The car also needs an awful lot of it, so much that at the end of the run Bloodhound will weigh **1.5 tonnes** less than it did at the start. And because the fuel has to be pumped into the car at such a rapid rate – around forty litres per second – it needs yet another engine. This one is borrowed from a Jaguar sports car, a supercharged five-litre V8 which is so powerful that it could fill a bathtub with the deadly fuel in under three seconds.

Slowing down is as dangerous and difficult as driving at supersonic speeds so the car has multiple braking systems as well as multiple engines. The first thing the driver has to do after hitting **1,000 mph** is take his foot off the accelerator. As the car slows down to just **800 mph**, a pair of gigantic carbon-fibre flaps known as air-brakes

At 600 mph a parachute is used to slow the car down.

pop out by the rear wheels. At **600 mph** a parachute is used to slow the car down further still, and at **400 mph** a second parachute can be used if necessary. The car's actual brakes don't begin to work until it has come down to **200 mph**, and even then it takes about five miles for the car finally to come to a halt.

Bloodhound is still undergoing final tests but when it is ready it will be transported to South Africa. Once there the record attempt will take place on a twelve-mile strip of the Kalahari Desert called the Hakskeenpan. The ground has already been prepared by **300** people employed to pick up **16,000 tonnes** of stones. Working mostly by hand, the job has taken several months but it means the scene is now set for the first ever **1,000 mph** car . . .

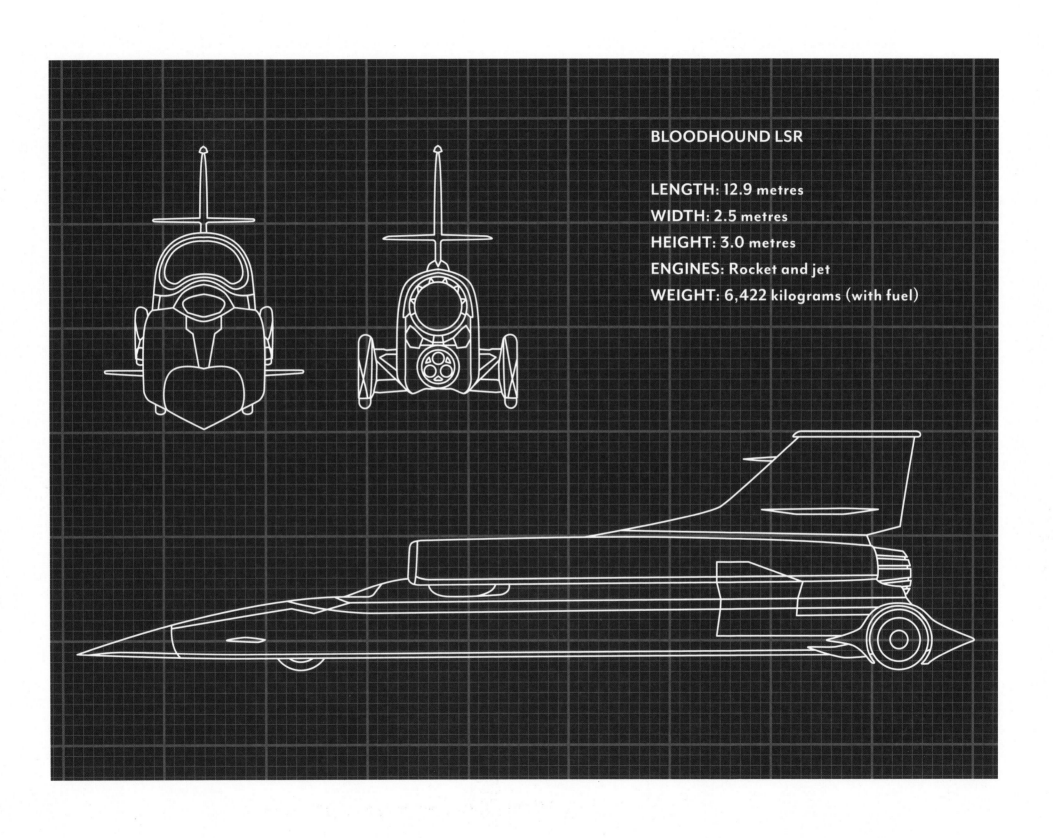

BLOODHOUND LSR

LENGTH: 12.9 metres

WIDTH: 2.5 metres

HEIGHT: 3.0 metres

ENGINES: Rocket and jet

WEIGHT: 6,422 kilograms (with fuel)

TUNNEL

BORING

MACHINE

TUNNEL BORING MACHINE

LONDON'S BIGGEST BORE

» **£10 million each, but barely faster than a snail**

» **Longer than fourteen double-deckers**

» **Helped to shift 4.5 million tonnes of soil**

London has the world's first and oldest underground passenger railway network, but also one of its newest lines. Trains began running under London in 1863, more than a century and a half ago, and the new Elizabeth Line is due to be opened in 2021.

When work began on this in 2009, the need to dig twenty-six miles of new tunnel made it one of Europe's largest and most expensive engineering projects. Building the new line involved **10,000** people working at forty different sites, and over a period of nearly ten years, an incredible **4,500,000 tonnes** of earth had to be dug out and taken to Essex where it was used to create a massive new nature reserve.

Most of the really heavy digging was done by eight giant tunnel boring machines (TBMs). These **£10 million** monsters are **148 metres** from nose to tail and weigh a thousand tonnes. That means each one is longer than fourteen double-decker buses parked end to end, and heavier than five blue whales, the largest animals that ever lived.

They have to be extremely powerful to cut through the earth but they are very slow. Most inched their way forward at just under **0.00037 miles per hour**, or about the same as a snail crossing a garden path. At that speed it would take nearly a week to travel **100 metres**, the same distance an Olympic sprinter covers in less than ten seconds. Even so, digging a tunnel using a TBM is still much quicker than doing it by hand, which is how the first railway lines were constructed under Victorian London.

If you could see a TBM working underground it would look a bit like a giant, cylindrical, robot caterpillar. At one end is a sharp, rotating cutting wheel (or cutterhead) and

Each one is longer than fourteen double-decker buses and heavier than five blue whales, the largest animals that ever lived.

at the other a series of linked trailers containing all the mechanical and electrical equipment needed to make it work. Conveyor belts take the waste from the front to the rear, mostly a mixture of chalk, gravel and muddy clay. Each TBM worked twenty-four hours a day, seven days a week, and had its own small kitchen and bathroom so that the operating team of twenty men and women could stay underground all day.

Once the chalk, gravel and clay had been removed, the new tunnel was reinforced using special strengthened concrete segments. More than **200,000** of these had to be lifted into place by the TBMs before being bolted into position.

With so many tunnels under London already, as well as sewers, pipes, electrical wiring, building foundations and other obstructions, each machine's movements had to be very carefully controlled. Special laser guidance systems made it possible for the teams to ensure their machines stayed on course from start to finish. Absolute precision was vital because at one point one of the new tunnels passes within **80 cm** of a Tube station.

Creeping forward in this way, the TBM crews made some incredible discoveries. The most gruesome was thousands of skulls and skeletons from several old cemeteries and medieval plague pits they found along the way. Many belonged to people who had died in the Black Death, and some showed signs of terrible injuries. Other finds included Roman horseshoes, flint tools from the Stone Age, a Tudor bowling ball, more than **13,000** Victorian pickle pots, and a pair of medieval ice skates with blades made from animal bones.

Too big to bring back up to the surface, all eight tunnel boring machines are still buried deep under London.

The machines were constructed in Germany but given English names when they arrived in London. The first pair were named Ada and Phyllis after two amazing women. Ada Lovelace was a brilliant mathematician who wrote the world's first computer program nearly **200** years ago. Phyllis Pearsall spent years walking more than **3,000 miles** around London. Along the way she checked off the names of **23,000** different streets before using this information to create the first accurate road map of the capital.

Now though, these and the other six machines are lost for ever. The TBMs were simply too big to bring back up to the surface once they had finished their work. Instead the crews set the controls so that each multi-million pound machine could dig one last tunnel and then bury itself deep under London. All eight are still down there somewhere, and will never be used again.

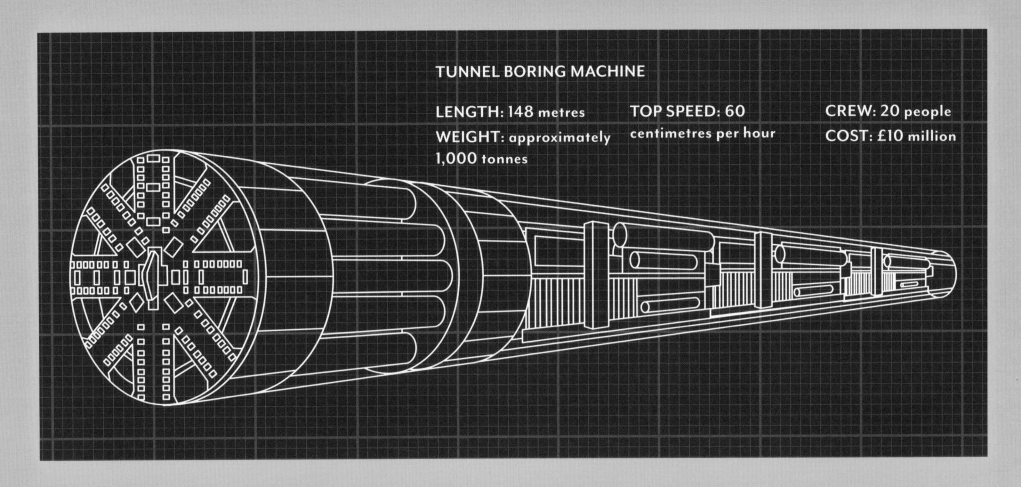

TUNNEL BORING MACHINE

LENGTH: 148 metres
WEIGHT: approximately 1,000 tonnes

TOP SPEED: 60 centimetres per hour

CREW: 20 people
COST: £10 million

WAYMO

THE CAR THAT STEERS ITSELF

» Knows where to go and how to get there

» Sensors 'look' nearly 300 metres in every direction

» The driver can watch TV, read a book – or even sleep

It's nearly **125** years since a French Panhard entered the Paris–Rouen Rally and finished in fourth place. Alfred Vacheron's little car is famous because it was the first one ever to have a steering wheel. It also had four wheels, a petrol engine, and pedals to control its speed and gears.

In other words, it was pretty much like the cars you see all the time. It was slower and it looked old-fashioned, but in every important respect it was much like the cars everyone drives today. Modern ones are more comfortable. They are safer and faster and a lot less polluting, but most still need an engine, pedals to make them go faster or stop, and a steering wheel to change direction.

Now Google is hoping to change all that with its Waymo. The Waymo is an entirely new kind of car, because it's designed to be autonomous. This means it doesn't need pedals or a steering wheel or even a driver. The owner sits in it like they would a normal car but doesn't need to do anything. The car knows where it is meant to go and how to get there. Anyone travelling in it can read a book, or watch a film or a television programme. They could even go to sleep and be woken up by the car when it reaches the destination.

Instead of relying on humans to control their speed and direction, autonomous cars use computer sensors and intelligent software. Google says the technology fitted to Waymo means it can 'see' **274 metres** in every direction. This enables the computers to work out where the car is and to see where it's going. The same technology is also meant to prevent the car from colliding with anything along the way, including objects such as kerbs and signposts, as well as pedestrians, cyclists and other vehicles.

Waymo is an entirely new kind of car, because it's designed to be autonomous. This means it doesn't even need a driver.

Lots of people really enjoy driving but many don't. The Waymo would be ideal for them, as well as or for anyone with a disability that prevents them from driving. It would also be great for anyone who wants to spend time doing something more useful than steering, speeding up and slowing down, or looking for somewhere to park.

The idea of a car with no controls might sound a bit scary, but the designers say they are confident they can engineer machines which are safer than human drivers. It's a shocking fact that more than thirty million people have been killed by cars since Karl Benz's invention first took to the streets of Germany (see page 6). This suggests humans may not be quite as good at driving as we like to think we are, and that it might be time for machines to take over.

They have covered more than two million miles in an attempt to show that driverless cars will one day be as safe and reliable as normal ones.

Well, maybe soon. At the moment the Waymo isn't for sale and even if it were it would not be allowed on the road in most countries. Before that can happen new laws are needed to decide who is responsible if an autonomous car is involved in an accident. You can't blame the driver if a car is driverless – but someone has to pay for the damage.

The car shown here is an experimental prototype. For the time being it is only able to travel at **25 mph** or less, and even if you could buy one it would be very, very expensive because of all the new technology it has. Prototypes like this have only been used for trials in parts of America. In that time they have covered more than two million miles in an attempt to show that driverless cars will one day be as safe and as reliable as normal ones.

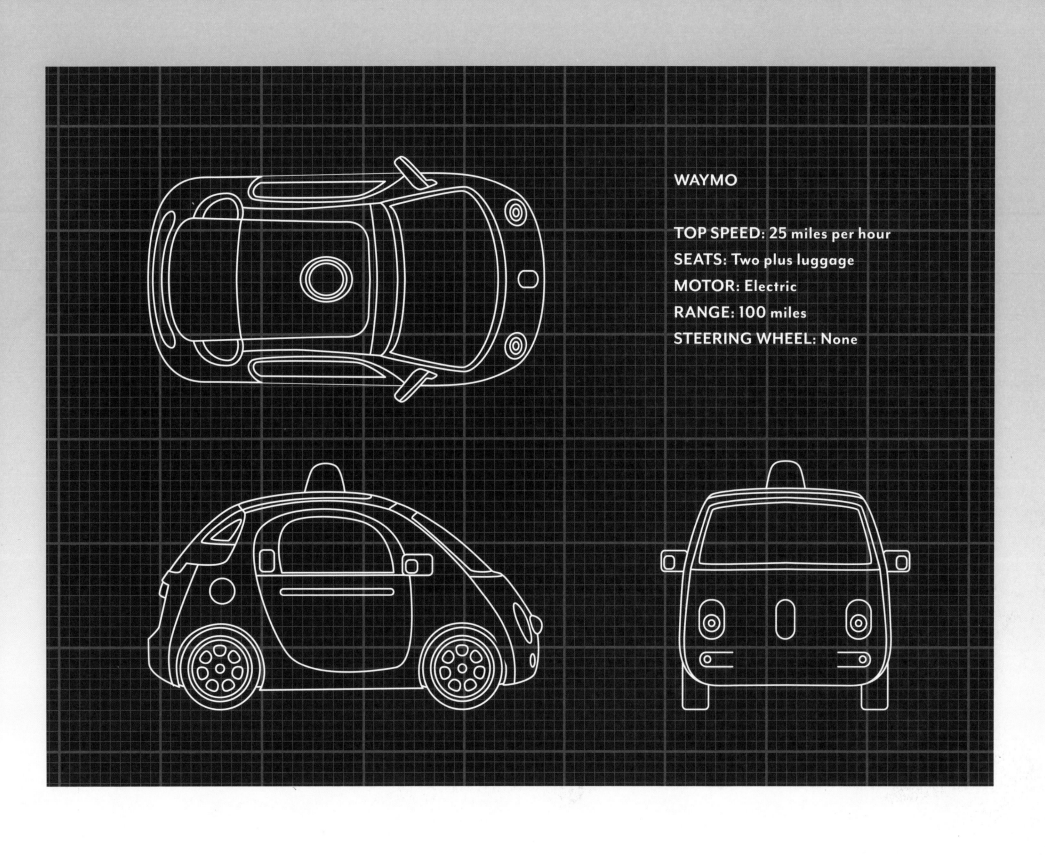

WAYMO

TOP SPEED: 25 miles per hour

SEATS: Two plus luggage

MOTOR: Electric

RANGE: 100 miles

STEERING WHEEL: None

SCALED COMPOSITES

STRA

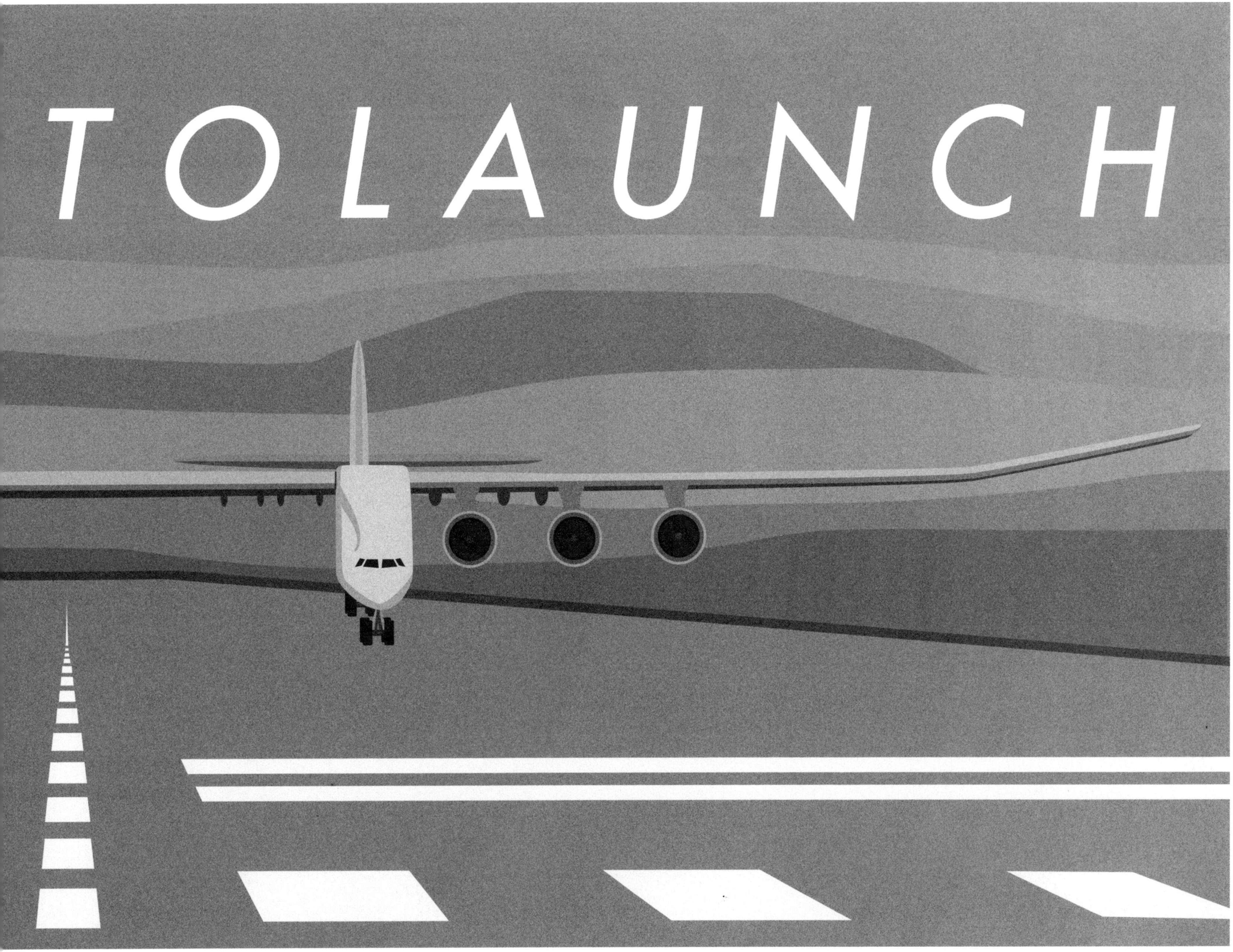
TOLAUNCH

STRATOLAUNCH

A PLANE FOR LAUNCHING ROCKETS

» **Twenty-eight wheels and six engines**

» **An aircraft designed to carry a rocket**

» **. . . And then to launch it into space!**

The American Stratolaunch is one of the strangest aircraft ever constructed. It looks like two huge airliners welded together. To take off it needs twenty-eight wheels and the largest wingspan of any aeroplane ever flown.

The jet engines it uses are the same as the ones fitted to the Boeing 747-400 airliner, one of the biggest jumbo jets. With room for **660** passengers and crew, it needs only four engines, but the Stratolaunch needs six even though it carries no passengers at all and has a crew of only three.

The Stratolaunch was being paid for by a computer industry billionaire, and the prototype is being built at a special spaceport out in California's Mojave Desert. It's been designed with just one job in mind: to launch a new type of spacecraft in an entirely novel way.

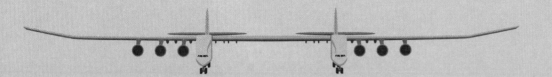

Normal rockets take off from the ground, which uses huge amounts of fuel and involves many dangers and technical difficulties for the crew. Now the idea is to create a new generation of rockets which can be launched in mid-air. The thinner atmosphere at high altitude makes it easier for the rocket to fly really, really fast. To get there it needs help from the Stratolaunch, which will take off and land using a runway like a normal airliner.

Before taking off the rocket is attached to Stratolaunch's wing, hung between its twin fuselages. This explains its strange appearance and why it has to be such an enormous aeroplane. The aircraft's pilot, co-pilot and flight engineer all sit in the cockpit of the right-hand fuselage, much like

in a normal jet. The rest of the space is needed for carrying fuel, more than **110 tonnes** of it.

Once the two machines have reached a height of about six miles, the pilot of the Stratolaunch releases the rocket so that the crew of the rocket can fire its engines and soar away into space. Many experts think this will be easier and cheaper than launching a rocket from the ground, but no one has tried it yet. It should certainly use a lot less fuel, although like any new technology it is taking a long time to get the details sorted out.

The idea is to create a new generation of rockets which can be launched in mid-air.

Travelling into space and back the rockets could be used for delivering satellites into orbit or for transporting astronauts to and from the International Space Station. If the technology works similar rockets could even make it possible for ordinary people like you and me to enjoy the thrilling experience of seeing what Earth looks like from space. It's a very daring plan and one that has already cost millions of dollars, although no one knows yet whether it will actually work.

With a rocket attached to it and all that fuel, the Stratolaunch weighs an incredible **589 tonnes**. That's more than twice the weight of even the largest airliner. This is why it needs six engines to get airborne, and why

The Stratolaunch weighs an incredible 589 tonnes – more than twice the weight of even the largest airliner.

it needs to carry so much fuel (which of course makes it even heavier). It also explains those huge wings, which stretch **117.4 metres** from tip to tip. That's considerably longer than the distance between the two goalmouths on a football pitch.

The first Stratolaunch has been completed and is now going through a long and expensive testing process. No one can pretend it is elegant or good-looking but when it takes off for its exciting, first ever flight it is sure to be an extraordinary sight.

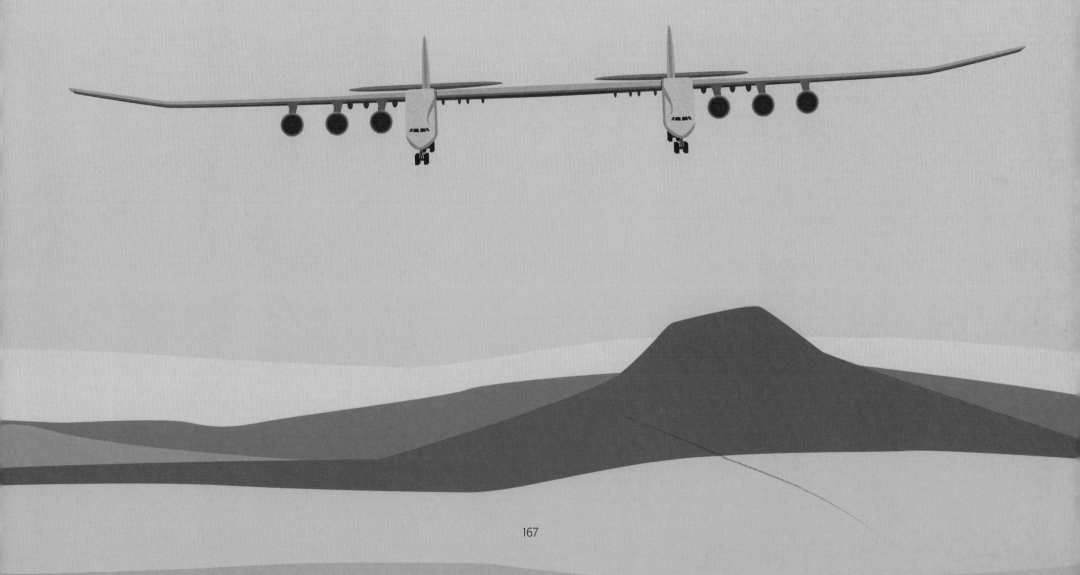

PAL-V

LIBERTY

PAL-V LIBERTY

A CAR THAT FLIES, A PLANE THAT DRIVES

» **112 mph on the road or in the air**

» **Room for two on board**

» **The first flying car to go on sale**

For almost as long as people have been driving around in machines, inventors have been trying to make cars that can fly. The benefits are obvious. There's far less traffic up there, and getting around would be so much quicker if you could fly in a straight line to your friend's house instead of following a road as it winds this way and that through the countryside.

For a long time neither cars nor aeroplanes were good enough to make such a thing even slightly possible. But technology gradually began to improve and about seventy years ago the first experimental designs took to the air. Most of these were small cars fitted with wings and a propeller, or small aircraft which could be driven on the road once the wings had been unbolted and removed. Unfortunately none of them worked very well, either as cars or as aeroplanes, and after one of them crashed into a horse the idea failed to take off.

Some enthusiasts refused to give up, however, and one of the latest designs for a flying car is the PAL-V Liberty, which comes from the Netherlands. The name is short for Personal Air and Land Vehicle, and it doesn't look much like a car or an aeroplane. In fact, it looks more like a sinister robot insect when it is driving along the road, and even more like one when it takes to the air.

Instead of wings the Liberty has a propeller at the back and large rotor blades on the roof a bit like those on a helicopter. The rotor blades aren't powered like a helicopter's but instead spin round automatically as the machine moves forward. When this happens the rotors begin to work like a kind of revolving wing. This enables the machine to take off but unlike a proper helicopter it needs a runway to do this and it can't hover. Once airborne though, and with the pilot and passenger seated one behind the other, it can fly at **112 mph** for about two hours before it needs to land and refuel.

Down on the ground the rotor blades are easy to fold back, and the propeller and tail fins slide out of the way behind the slim body. Now it is ready to be driven along the road like a three-wheeled sports car, although it is rather noisy. It also leans over like a motorbike when it goes around a bend, which can feel a bit scary if the passenger isn't expecting it.

Anyone legally allowed to drive a normal car is able to drive the Liberty along the road (the controls are quite similar) but owners need a pilot's licence before they can take off and fly. It's a lot narrower than a car so it looks like it would be good for driving around in city traffic, but it is very expensive. The cost of each one is around **£500,000**, which means that for the same money you could have a Lamborghini *and* a Rolls-Royce instead – and still have enough change to buy a small aeroplane.

AFTERWORD

Whether they're designed for land, sea or air, few things provide a more exciting demonstration of human inventiveness and creativity than a machine.

Some of the most remarkable inventions are the result of a sudden burst of inspiration. When Karl Benz built the world's first motor car, most people went everywhere on foot or on horseback and probably had no idea what his invention was even for. Others took years to design and required incredible teamwork, like America's gigantic moon rocket, the Saturn V. This required billions of dollars and the expertise of hundreds of thousands of men and women before it was possible to send the first three humans to another world.

Machines don't have to be successful to be interesting, however. London's first electric taxis, for example, were even slower than a horse and cart, and they quickly went out of business. At the other end of the scale the rocket-powered Komet 163 was at least **100 mph** faster than any other World War II fighter, but it used so much fuel and so quickly that after three minutes the doomed pilot had none left to fly with.

More recently, the Spanish navy's new submarine was described as one of the most advanced anywhere in the world, but the prototype weighed **100 tonnes** more than expected and it quickly sank. Incredibly they had to make the next one even bigger in order to get it to float . . .

But on the other hand the most successful machines can lead to the creation of a whole new industry. Within a few years of Karl Benz's first, short journey in his new automobile, hundreds of workshops and small factories began building rival models of their own. Today the motor industry provides jobs for millions of people around the world, and cars have given us greater freedom to move around than anyone in the past could even have dreamed of.

What the future holds, nobody knows. Even larger and more powerful rockets than the Saturn V could eventually enable people to travel deeper into the solar system. Personal helicopters or submarines could one day be almost as common as cars. And eventually another Karl Benz could come along and in a similar blinding flash of inspiration invent a machine which suddenly changes everything, for everyone, all over again.

GLOSSARY

ACCELERATE – speeding up.

AERODYNAMIC – a smooth shape enabling a machine to travel efficiently through the air.

ALTITUDE – a machine's height above ground.

AUTOMOBILE – another name for a motor car.

AUTONOMOUS – a machine that is able to work without a driver or operator.

AVRO VULCAN – a British nuclear bomber.

AXLE – a rod attached to a vehicle and passing through the centre of each wheel.

BODYWORK – the main, external part of a car.

BONNET – the engine cover of a car.

CANNON – a large gun.

CAPSULE – the part of a space rocket housing the crew.

CATAPULT – a device for firing objects (for example at a castle).

CATERPILLAR TRACKS – a series of heavy metal links passing around the wheels of a vehicle designed to cross rough ground.

Cc – cubic centimetre.

COCKPIT – that part of an aircraft where the pilot sits.

COMPONENT – another word for a part of a machine.

CONVEYOR BELT – a continuous, moving belt for moving parts in a factory.

CRANE – a machine for lifting heavy objects.

CRUISE MISSILE – a missile able to be fired accurately over huge distances.

CYLINDER – part of an engine in which air and fuel mix to provide power.

DECKS – the different storeys on a ship.

DRONE – a pilotless, remote control aircraft used in modern warfare.

FORMULA ONE (F1) – the fastest class of single-seater racing car.

FUSELAGE – the body of an aircraft.

GALLON – a traditional measure of fuel, equivalent to approximately 4.5 litres.

GLIDER – an aeroplane with no engine.

GRAND PRIX – a motor race.

HANGAR – a large building used for housing aircraft when they are not flying.

HORSEPOWER – a way of describing the power of a car or other vehicle.

HULL – the main body of a ship or boat.

JET – a type of aircraft engine which replaced traditional propellers.

JOYSTICK – pilots use joysticks to control the speed and direction of aircraft.

LOCOMOTIVE – the part of a railway train that pulls the carriages along.

MPH – miles per hour.

NOZZLE – a cylindrical spout at the end of a pipe.

PEDAL – foot controls used in cars and aircraft.

PROPELLER – a spinning device attached to an engine enabling aircraft and ships to move forwards.

PROTOTYPE – the first version of a new machine designed to show whether or not it works.

RADAR – an electronic system used to locate approaching aircraft and other machines long before they can be seen.

RIVETS – a short pin, usually of metal, which is used to fix two large items together.

ROTOR BLADE – a sort of large propeller fitted to helicopters.

RUDDER – a hinged plate used to steer an aircraft, ship or boat.

SATELLITE – an unmanned spaceship which orbits the Earth. Used for communication and collecting information.

SHELL – an explosive device fired by large artillery guns and tanks.

SHERMAN TANK – one of the most successful armoured vehicles of World War II.

SQUADRON – a group of military aircraft or warships.

STEM – the front of a ship, where the two sides of the hull join together.

STERN – the rear of a ship.

STOREYS – the name given to the separate floors of a house or other building.

STREAMLINE – to make a machine aerodynamic (see above).

SUPERSONIC – a machine that flies faster than the speed of sound, so more than 767 miles per hour.

TANKER – a ship designed to carry huge quantities of liquid.

THERMONUCLEAR WEAPON – another name for the most destructive type of bomb.

TILLER – a device used for moving the rudder (see above) on a ship or boat.

TITANIUM – a type of metal which is light but strong.

TONNE – a weight equivalent to 1000 kilograms.

TURBOCHARGED – the process of forcing air into an engine to make it even more powerful.

TURBULENCE – a patch of fast-moving air that can make flying uncomfortable or even dangerous.

WAGON – another name for a cart pulled by horses.